THE CRUISE OF THE
DAINTY

ROVINGS IN THE PACIFIC

W. H. G. KINGSTON

1st WORLD
LIBRARY
Literary Society

The Cruise of the Dainty

W. H. G. Kingston

© 1st World Library, 2007
PO Box 2211
Fairfield, IA 52556
www.1stworldlibrary.com
First Edition

LCCN: 2007934210

Softcover ISBN: 978-1-4218-9682-3
Hardcover ISBN: 978-1-4218-9782-0
eBook ISBN: 978-1-4218-9582-6

Purchase *"The Cruise of the Dainty"*
as a traditional bound book at:
www.1stWorldLibrary.com/purchase.asp?ISBN=978-1-4218-9682-3

1st World Library is a literary, educational organization
dedicated to:

- Creating a free internet library of downloadable ebooks

- Hosting writing competitions and offering book publishing
scholarships.

Interested in more 1st World Library books? contact:
literacy@1stworldlibrary.com
Check us out at: www.1stworldlibrary.com

1st World Library Literary Society

Giving Back to the World

"If you want to work on the core problem, it's early school literacy."

- James Barksdale, former CEO of Netscape

"No skill is more crucial to the future of a child, or to a democratic and prosperous society, than literacy."

- Los Angeles Times

"Literacy... means far more than learning how to read and write... The aim is to transmit... knowledge and promote social participation."

- UNESCO

"Literacy is not a luxury, it is a right and a responsibility. If our world is to meet the challenges of the twenty-first century we must harness the energy and creativity of all our citizens."

- President Bill Clinton

"Parents should be encouraged to read to their children, and teachers should be equipped with all available techniques for teaching literacy, so the varying needs and capacities of individual kids can be taken into account."

- Hugh Mackay

CHAPTER ONE

"Never was bothered with a more thorough calm!" exclaimed my brother Harry, not for the first time that morning, as he and I, in spite of the sweltering heat, paced the deck of our tight little schooner the *Dainty*, then floating motionless on the smooth bosom of the broad Pacific. The empty sails hung idly from the yards. The dog-vanes imitated their example. Not the tiniest wavelet disturbed the shining surface of the ocean, not a cloud dimmed the intense blue of the sky, from which the sun glared forth with a power that made the pitch in the seams of the deck bubble up and stick to the soles of our feet, and though it might have failed to cook a beefsteak in a satisfactory manner, was rapidly drying some strings of fish hung up in the rigging.

The white men of the crew were gathered forward, in such shade as they could find, employed under the superintendence of Tom Platt, our mate, in manufacturing mats, sinnet, rope yarns, or in knotting and splicing; the dark-skinned natives, of whom we had several on board similarly engaged, were mostly on the other side of the deck, apparently indifferent as to whether they were in the shade or sunshine. Even my brother, the commander of the *Dainty*, was too impatient to think much about the broiling we were undergoing, as we walked from the taffrail to a short distance before the mainmast, where we invariably turned to face back again; while during the intervals in our conversation, from an old habit, he whistled vehemently for a breeze, not that in consequence he really expected it to come.

As we walked with our faces forward I was amused by watching old Tom, who, marline-spike in hand, was stropping a block, now inspecting the work of one man, now that of another, and then giving his attention to a lad, seated on the spars stowed under the long-boat, engaged in splicing an eye to the end of a rope.

"Is this all right, Mr Platt?" asked the lad, handing the rope to the mate, who, squirting a mouthful of tobacco juice over the bulwarks, turned it round and round to examine it critically.

"Ay, t'will do, Dick—wants scraping a bit; let's see how you'll serve it," answered old Tom, giving back the rope.

After taking a few more turns my brother stopped. "Do you think, Platt, that, we shall be long delayed by this provoking calm?" he asked.

"Can't say, Cap'en. Known such to last for the better part of a week in these latitudes," answered the mate, coming a few steps aft. "Maybe, though, we'll get a breeze to-morrow, maybe not."

"We are not likely to get it yet, at all events, from the look of the sky," said Harry. "We'll rig the awning and persuade Mary and Fanny to come on deck. They'll be better here than in the close cabin." Just as he spoke Nat Amiel, his young brother-in-law, appeared at the companion-hatch.

"Wanted to see if you were asleep, as we have been below all the morning," he exclaimed. "Well, I declare, it is hot, though it's baking enough in the cabin to satisfy a salamander."

W. H. G. Kingston

"We'll soon have some more shade, and then ask the ladies to come on deck and enjoy it," I answered. "In the meantime hand up a couple of the folding-chairs, and I'll place some gratings for them to put their feet on."

Nat dived into the cabin, and the mate calling the men aft we quickly had an awning rigged to cover the after-part of the deck. Harry then went below to bring up his wife and her sister. They were by this time pretty well accustomed to a sea life, as three weeks had passed since we left Brisbane in Queensland. My brother Harry, who had been a lieutenant in the navy, had about four years before come out to settle in the colony, being engaged at the time to Miss Mary Amiel, the eldest daughter of an English clergyman. Agricultural pursuits had not been much to his taste, and he had therefore settled himself in Brisbane for the purpose of carrying on a mercantile business. He had made a very fair commence-ment, and had returned about a year before the time I am speaking of to marry his intended. On his arrival he found that Mr Amiel had died, and that his family, consisting of another daughter and a son, were left in very poor circumstances. Prompted by his generous feelings, he at once invited Fanny and Nat to return with him and his bride to the colony. This they gladly agreed to do, and the whole party forthwith took a passage on board an emigrant ship, which after a prosperous voyage reached the colony.

I had from my earliest days wished to go to sea, and my mother having consented, as I could not obtain a nomination for the *Britannia*, I got a berth as a midshipman on board a trader bound for China. I was unfortunate in my ship and my captain. This gave me a dislike not so much to the sea as to the merchant service, and on my return from my first voyage, finding that my brother, to whom I was much attached, had gone back to Queensland, I got leave from my mother, after representing to her the sort of life I had been leading, to go and join him, she being certain that he would be very glad to receive me.

As I had made the best use of my opportunities of becoming a seaman during my first voyage, I had no difficulty in obtaining a berth on board a ship bound to Queensland, called the *Eclipse*, commanded by Captain Archer, and I was thus able to work my passage out free of expense. On this occasion also I made good use of my time, by adding considerably to my knowledge of seamanship, and by studying navigation. Though I was before the mast, as I had my own sextant and books the officers allowed me to take observations with them and to keep the ship's reckoning, I had thus a right, with the experience I had had, to consider myself a fair seaman.

The *Eclipse* had been four days at sea, when the third mate summoned me to accompany him into the forehold to get up some casks of provisions. While searching for those he wanted, I heard a sound as if some one was gasping for breath, and then a low moan. I told the mate.

"What can that be, sir?" I asked. "It comes from forward."

"Take the lantern, and see if there is any one there," he answered.

I made my way to the spot whence I fancied the sounds proceeded, and lowering my lantern into a small hole, I saw the figure of a boy crouching down, with his head resting against a cask. He made no movement, and his eyes appeared to be closed.

"There's some one here, sir," I cried out. "He seems to be very far gone."

W. H. G. Kingston

The mate quickly joined me. "A young stowaway!" he exclaimed. "We must have him on deck at once, or it will be beyond the doctor's skill to bring him round. I have known more than one lad lose his life in this way; and I shall get blamed for not having examined the hold before we left port."

Saying this he lifted the lad in his arms while I held the lantern, and forthwith carried him on deck. The low groans the boy uttered showed us that he was still alive, but he was pale as death and in a wretched condition. He was dressed like a respectable lad, but his face and clothes were covered with dirt.

"The captain will be in a great taking when he finds this out," said the mate; "still more so if the young fellow dies. Go aft, Ned, and call the doctor; maybe he'll be able to bring him round."

I hurried aft, and soon found the surgeon, who was in his dispensary. When I told him what he was wanted for, he at once, bringing some medicine with him, hurried forward.

"This will do him good," he said, pouring some liquid down the lad's throat. "I don't think, Mr Simmons, that you need be anxious about him."

The young stowaway almost immediately opened his eyes and stared about him. The doctor then ordered the cook to get some broth ready, while two of the women passengers brought some warm water and washed the poor lad's face and hands. The broth, which he eagerly swallowed, revived him still more, and the doctor considered that he had sufficiently recovered to be conveyed to the sick bay, the women offering to stay by his side and to give him medicine and food as he might require them.

"If he is carefully tended he may come round," said the doctor; "but had he remained another hour in the hold I feel pretty sure that he would have lost his life."

Having been the means of discovering the young stowaway, I felt a certain amount of interest in him, and, whenever I could, went in to see how he was getting on. The next day he had so far recovered as to be able to speak without difficulty. He told me that his name was Richard Tilston, though he was generally called Dick by his friends; that he had had a great longing for going to sea; and that, as his father would not let him, he had run off from school, and found his way down to the docks. Hearing that our ship was to haul out into the stream early the next day, he waited until late in the evening, when he stole on board, and had, without being discovered, got down into the hold. He had brought a bottle of water and some biscuits, together with a couple of sausages. Supposing that the ship would at once put to sea, he had not placed himself on an allowance, and in less than three days had exhausted all his provisions and water. As the sea was smooth he fancied that we were still in the river, and was therefore afraid to creep out, until he became too ill and weak to do so.

From the tone of his voice and the way he expressed himself I suspected that he was a young gentleman, but I did not like to ask questions, and waited to hear what account he would give of himself. He was, however, too ill to say much, and was in a great fright at hearing that the captain would be very angry with him for having stowed himself away. I tried to reassure him by saying I did not believe that the captain was as yet made acquainted with his being on board, and, as far as I could judge, he was a good-natured man, and would probably not say much to him.

In spite of all the doctor's care and the nursing he received

W. H. G. Kingston

from the two kind women who had taken him in charge, it was considerably more than a week before he was able to get up and move about the deck. When his clothes had been cleaned and he himself had been well washed, he looked a very respectable lad.

At last, one day, Captain Archer saw him, and inquired who he was. The third mate had to confess all about the matter, and the captain then sent for Dick, and in an angry tone asked what had induced him to come on board.

"I wanted to go to sea, sir, and didn't know any other way of managing it," answered Dick.

"You took a very bad way, and nearly lost your life in carrying out your foolish notion," said the captain. "You have been pretty severely punished by what you have gone through, or I should have given you a sound flogging; as it is, I intend to let you off, but you will understand you must make yourself useful on board and try to pay for your passage; I can have no idlers, remember, and you will get thrashed if you do not work. I will speak to the mates about you, and they'll see that you have something to do."

Poor Dick, looking very much ashamed of himself, returned forward. The mates took care that he should have something to do, and the men also, for Dick was at everybody's beck and call, and had to do all sorts of dirty and disagreeable work. When there was no other work for him he was employed by the cook to sweep out the caboose and clean the pots and pans. He now and then got his back up, when he received a rope's-ending for his pains. I did the best I could for him, but often could not save him from ill-treatment, and at last, in the bitterness of his soul, he complained that he was leading a regular dog's life, and that he heartily wished he had not come to sea.

"I won't stand it any longer," he exclaimed. "I'll jump overboard and drown myself."

"Don't even talk of doing so wicked and foolish a thing," I said. "You wished to become a sailor, now that you have the opportunity of learning your duty you do nothing but grumble and complain. You must take the rough and the smooth together. I wasn't over well off on my first voyage, though my mother had paid a premium to the owners and I was on the quarterdeck, but I saw while I remained on board that there was no use complaining, so I took things as they were, and by keeping my eyes open and my wits awake became in a short time a fair seaman."

Poor Dick said that he would try to follow my advice, but he, notwithstanding, would answer when spoken to, and consequently I was unable to save him from ill-treatment, as he had brought it down upon himself.

During a heavy gale we encountered, when near the latitude of the Cape, one of the so-called midshipmen fell overboard and was drowned. The captain knowing that I could take an observation, and hearing that I was able to keep accounts and would be useful to him, invited me to take the poor fellow's berth. This, though it gave me a good deal of work, I was very glad to do, and I thus saw much less than before of Dick. As I was well treated I soon regained my old affection for a sea life, and had half determined to return home in the ship should my brother not especially press me to remain. When, however, we arrived at Brisbane, and Harry told me of his contemplated trip, and that he should be very glad of my assistance, I kept to my former intention of remaining with him. I therefore wished Captain Archer and his ship, the *Eclipse*, good-bye, and took up my quarters with Harry and his family. I liked Mary and her sister, whom I had not before seen, very much, and I was glad that Harry had not taken them into the bush, for they did not appear at all suited to the rough style of life they would have had to lead there, for they were both very pretty and elegant, and had never been accustomed to hard work, though they now did their best to make themselves useful in the house, and were never idle. Their brother, Nat, was a capital little fellow—as merry as a cricket and never out of temper, even when his face and hands were bitten all over by mosquitoes, or when the pugnacious insects were buzzing round us in thousands, and that is a trial to the sweetest of tempers. We used to have music and reading in the evenings, and very pleasant evenings they were—indeed, we lived much as we should have done in the old country. Altogether, I congratulated myself that I had decided on stopping out.

My brother was, however, somewhat anxious about the state of business. "You see, Ned, there is not, I fear, much to be done at present," he said. "I have, therefore, thought of making the trip I spoke to you about. A number of vessels sail from Sydney and other places to collect cargoes of palm-oil and sandal-wood, and some few go in search of pearls. They do not all trade honestly with the natives, and several have suffered in consequence, their crews having been attacked and murdered; but I hope, by trading honestly and by being always on my guard against surprise, to make a profitable venture. I have an especial reason for wishing to sail at once, as the day before your arrival I received information from an old shipmate of mine, Tom Platt, of the existence of a small group of islands, among which pearls of large size are obtained by the natives in unusual abundance. Tom, who has been out in these seas for some years on board whalers and other craft, sailed a few months ago in a small schooner, the *Zebra*, from Sydney. Both master and crew were rough, lawless fellows, and Tom told me that he often wished himself clear of them, but they touched at no place where he could venture to land till they reached the islands I speak of. Here the master, for his own purposes, at first behaved better to the natives than he was accustomed to do, as he wanted to obtain some pigs, cocoanuts, and other provisions. They consequently, without hesitation, came on board in considerable numbers. Many of them were observed to wear necklaces of white beads, which the captain supposed to be made of glass, and to have been obtained from some previous trader. On examining, however, one of the strings of beads, what was his surprise to find that they were pearls! Being a cunning fellow, he kept his discovery to himself till he had obtained all he could induce the natives to part with, when, though he fancied that he had made his fortune, he formed the design of kidnapping as many people as his schooner would hold, as an effectual way of preventing other traders from having any friendly intercourse with the islanders and discovering his secret, and thereby spoiling his market. Tom Platt was the only person among the crew who suspected what the white beads really were, and he managed, unknown to the captain, to obtain a necklace, which he hid in his pocket. The very evening before the natives were to have been seized a heavy gale sprang up, and the schooner was driven out to sea. Before many days had gone by she was cast away on an uninhabited island, when all hands, with the exception of Tom Platt, were lost. He supported existence on shell-fish and a few birds he knocked down, while a small cask of water washed ashore saved him from dying of thirst. Just as it was exhausted, he was taken off by a vessel bound for this place. I met him, looking very ill and wretched, wandering about the street the very day he landed. We recognised each other, and I took him to my house, where he became so much worse that, had it not been for the careful way he was nursed, I believe he would have died. He seemed to think so himself, and was very grateful. While I was sitting with him one day, having a yarn of old times, he gave me an account of the pearl islands, and assured me that he could find them again, having carefully

W. H. G. Kingston

noted the distance the schooner had run to the reef on which she was wrecked, as also its position on the chart. He then showed me the necklace, of which he had not spoken to any one. His narrative first put our proposed venture into my head. When I told him of my idea he at once agreed to accompanying me, saying that he should be content with any wages I could afford to give him. Though a first-rate seaman, he cannot be much of a navigator, so that had you, Ned, not come out I should have been obliged to get another mate; and now that you have come, we will forthwith commence our preparations."

"The first thing to be done is to find a suitable craft," I said.

"I have had my eye on one—a schooner, the *Dainty*, of a hundred and twenty tons, built for a fruit-trader, which was brought out here from England by a settler only a month ago," he answered.

"Then let us go at once and have a look at her, and, if she is in good condition, secure her," I exclaimed; for, after the account Harry had given me, I had become very eager to undertake the expedition.

We started forthwith. The *Dainty* was even more suited for our object than we had expected. She had well fitted up cabins, like those of a yacht, with a hold large enough for all the cargo and stores we might wish to stow—was well-found and in capital condition; so Harry at once made an offer for her, which being accepted, the *Dainty* became his.

In the evening Harry said what he had done.

"You do not intend to leave me behind, I hope," exclaimed Mary.

"Or me either," cried Miss Fanny Amiel. "What should we poor girls do all alone by ourselves in this little bakehouse?"

"You must let me go as cabin-boy," said Nat. "I'll make myself tremendously useful."

"I'll talk it over with Mary," answered Harry, who looked not at all ill pleased at the thoughts of having his wife to accompany him of her own free will. The result of the talk was that the next morning it was settled that we were all to go, the house and business being left in charge of a trust-worthy old clerk, Mr Simon Humby, who had accompanied Harry when he came out the first time from England. We were very busy for the next few days in making preparations for the voyage—the ladies in the house assisted by Nat, and Harry, and I in refitting the schooner—purchasing provisions, stores, and articles for bartering with the natives. We procured also four small brass guns, with some muskets, pistols, boarding-pikes, and cutlasses.

"We shall not, I hope, have to use them," said Harry. "But, now especially that we are to have ladies on board, we must be well prepared for defence should we be attacked."

It was easy enough to prepare the vessel for sea, but Harry expected to find some difficulty in securing an efficient crew. He of course at once applied to Tom Platt.

"I'll see about that, sir," he answered. "You mustn't be too particular as to what sort of chaps they may be, provided they are good seamen—for as to their characters, I'm not likely to be able to say much."

"Pick up the best you can find," said Harry. "They'll probably behave well enough, if kept under strict discipline."

Tom was as good as his word. In the course of a few days he had engaged ten hands—a strong crew for a vessel of the *Dainty's* size—six Englishmen, a New Zealander, a Sandwich Islander, and two blacks, natives of Tanna, an island of the New Hebrides Group. Tom confessed that he had more confidence in the probable good conduct of the Pacific islanders than he had in that of the white men, who, however, when they came on board, looked more decent fellows than I had expected.

Just as the schooner was ready for sea, Harry and I were one evening leaving the quay, when I saw a lad in ragged clothes, who, on catching sight of me, tried to hide himself behind a stack of planks lately landed. In spite of his forlorn and dirty condition, I recognised him as the young stowaway who had come out with me on board the *Eclipse*.

"Hillo, Dick Tilston, can that be you?" I exclaimed. "Come here. What have you been about?"

On being called, he approached, looking very sheepish.

"Now, don't be scolding at me," he said, taking my hand, which I held out to him. "You know how I was treated aboard the *Eclipse*. I couldn't stand it any longer, so when she was about to sail I slipped ashore, and hid away till she had gone. I've since been knocking about, unable to get any work, for no one will engage me without a character, as they guess that I'm a runaway, and take me for a young thief. I've sold my clothes and everything I had for food, and have got only these rags to cover me."

I knew that what Dick said was true. I asked him if he still wished to be a sailor, or would rather go up the country and seek for employment, which I was sure he would be able to obtain with my brother's recommendation.

"I would rather be a sailor than anything else, if I could serve under a good captain," he answered.

"Well, then, stop a moment, and I'll speak to my brother," I said; and I ran after Harry. I told him in a few words about Dick.

"Well, he may come with us," he said. "But he must try to make himself useful, and not fancy that he is a young gentleman to do what he likes."

I ran back to Dick. The poor fellow was delighted, and burst into tears. "I own, Ned, I've had nothing to eat all day in this land of plenty, for I could not bring myself to beg, and nobody offered me anything," he exclaimed, scarcely able for shame to get out his words.

I fortunately had a shilling in my pocket. "Here, Dick, go and get something to eat," I said, giving it to him. I thought that he would rather have some food first, before he came to talk with Harry. "Then come up to my brother's house—you can easily find it—and I will speak to him in the meantime." Dick promised to come.

While we walked home I told my brother more about Dick.

"It is very clear that the first thing we must do for him is to give him an outfit, or he'll not be presentable on board, and then I hope, from gratitude, that he will behave well," he observed.

On our way we stopped at an outfitter's, and Harry gave an order to the storekeeper to supply whatever I might select for Dick. As we walked on, he told me what things he wished me to get.

W. H. G. Kingston

Soon after we reached home Dick presented himself at the door, looking somewhat brighter than he did when I first saw him, but rather ashamed of himself and unwilling to come in. Harry, however, came and had a few words with him, and seemed satisfied that he might be made useful on board the schooner.

As we had no place to put him up in the house, he told me to get a lodging for him for the night, and to see that he had plenty of food. "I say, Ned," he added, "just give him a hint to take a bath and get his hair cut before he puts on his clean clothes."

Accordingly, telling Dick to come with me, I took him to the outfitter's. We soon got the necessary clothing for him, and then left him at a lodging with a person who knew my brother.

That evening was to be the last on shore for many a long day. Mary and her sister were in high spirits at the thoughts of their trip, for which they had got everything ready.

The next morning Dick presented himself so changed for the better in appearance, that Harry scarcely knew him. He looked a fine, intelligent sailor lad, and at once began to make himself useful in carrying down our things to the boat: most of our heavier luggage had been sent on board the previous evening. Mr Humby came off in a shore boat.

While our own boat was being hoisted in, my brother gave his last directions.

"I'll do my best, Mr Harry, and I pray that you may have a successful voyage, and when you return find all things going on well," he said, as he shook hands with us all.

The anchor was then hove up, and sail being made, we stood out of the harbour, while Mr Humby returned on shore, waving his last adieus.

The first part of our voyage was uneventful. We had fine weather, a fair wind, and a smooth sea, and the ladies soon got accustomed to their life on board, declaring that it was even more pleasant than they had expected, though they should like occasionally to get sight of some of the beautiful islands of the Pacific, of which they had so often heard.

We left New Caledonia and the Loyalty Islands on our port side, then steered to the north between the New Hebrides and the Fiji Islands, at neither of which my brother wished to touch.

Day after day we sailed on without sighting land, and at last Emily exclaimed, "What has become of the islands we have heard so much about? I thought we should not pass a day without seeing several of them. They appear on the chart to be very close together, like the constellations in the sky."

"But if you will measure off on the chart the distances they are apart, you will easily understand how it is we have sailed so far without seeing them," said Harry.

The very next day, as Fanny was looking over the starboard side, Harry pointed out to her several blue hillocks rising out of the ocean, which he told her were the northern islands of Fiji, the habitation of a dark-skinned race, once the most notorious cannibals in the Pacific.

"I am very glad to keep away from them, then," answered Fanny, "for I shouldn't at all like to run the risk of being captured and eaten."

"Not much chance of that," said Harry. "The larger number of them have given up their bad habits, and promise to become as civilised as any of the people in these seas."

"Still, I would rather not go near their shores," said Fanny.

She little thought at the time that there were many other islands in every direction, the inhabitants of which were quite as savage as those of Fiji had been.

From the first, Tom Platt had taken a fancy to Dick, who had hitherto behaved himself remarkably well.

"We'll make a seaman of the lad, if he only sticks to it," he said to me. "The rope's-endings, as he tells me he used to get aboard the *Eclipse*, did him a world of good, though he didn't think so."

I always treated Dick in a friendly way, though he was before the mast, and I was glad to find that he did not presume on this, but willingly did whatever he was ordered. Tom had had a hammock slung for Dick near his berth away from the men, whose conversation, he said, was not likely to do him any good.

Our life on board was very regular; Tom and I kept watch and watch, the crew being divided between us, while Harry, as captain, was on deck at all hours whenever he thought it necessary.

CHAPTER TWO

The calm which I described at the commencement of my narrative had continued for many hours, and when the sun sank beneath the horizon there was not the slightest sign of a coming breeze. It was my first watch, and before Harry went below he charged me to keep a careful look-out, and to call him should there be any sign of a change of weather. The schooner still floated motionless on the water; scarcely a sound was heard, except the cheeping of the main boom, and the low voices of the men forward, as they passed the watch spinning their oft-told yarns to each other.

I slowly paced the deck, enjoying the comparative coolness of the night, after the intense heat of the day. The stars in the southern hemisphere were shining brilliantly overhead, reflected in the mirror-like ocean. The watch at length were silent, and had apparently dropped off to sleep, though I could see the figure of the man on the look-out as he paced up and down or leaned over the bulwarks. Suddenly, the stillness was broken by a dull splash. I started; it seemed to me as if some one had fallen overboard, but it was only one of the monsters of the deep poking its snout for an instant above the surface, and when I looked over the side it had disappeared. Occasionally I heard similar sounds at various distances. I had some difficulty in keeping myself awake, though by continuing my walk I was able to do so; but I was not sorry when the old mate turned out, without being called, to relieve me.

"We have not got a breeze yet," I observed as he came on deck.

"No, Master Ned, and we shan't get one during my watch either; and maybe not when the sun is up again," he answered.

Tom was right. When I came on deck the next morning the sea was as calm as before. Though it appeared impossible that we could have moved our position, I was greatly surprised, on looking away to the westward, to see what I at first took to be the masts of a vessel rising above the horizon. I pointed them out to my brother who had just come on deck. He told me to go aloft with a telescope and examine them more minutely. I then discovered that they were trees growing on a small island, apparently cocoanuts, or palms of some sort. Beyond, to the south and west, were several islands of greater elevation, some blue and indistinct, but others appeared to be covered with trees like the nearer one, while between us and them extended from north to south a line of white surf distinctly marked on the blue ocean. On reporting to Harry what I had seen, he said that the surf showed the existence of a barrier reef surrounding the islands. "We may find a passage through it, but sometimes these reefs extend for miles without an opening through them. A strong current must be setting from the eastward towards it, or we should not have been drawn so far during the night, for certainly there was no appearance of an island in that direction at sundown."

We soon had convincing proof that Harry was right in his conjecture. There could be no doubt that a current was setting us towards the land, for the trees gradually rose higher and higher above the water, and at length we could see them from the deck, while the white line of surf breaking on the reef became more and more distinct. At the same time a slowly moving, at first scarcely perceptible swell, which Fanny called the breathing of the ocean, passed ever and anon under the vessel, lifting her so gently that the sails remained as motionless as before. It was difficult indeed to discover that there was any movement in the mirror-like surface of the deep, and yet we could feel the deck rise and fall under our feet. The awning was rigged, and Mary and Fanny were seated in their easy-chairs under it, Mary reading aloud while her sister worked. Nat, who had placed himself near them, cross-legged on a grating, to listen, with a marline-spike and a piece of rope, was practising the art of splicing, in which he had made fair progress. "I say, Ned, I wish you would show me how to work a Turk's head," he exclaimed.

I went to him and did as he asked me. This made Mary stop reading; and Fanny, looking out towards the island, remarked, "How near we are getting. I am so glad, for I want to see a real coral island, and that of course is one. I suppose we shall anchor when we get close to it, and be able to go on shore." Harry, who overheard her, made no reply, but looked unusually grave, and told me to bring the chart from below. Spreading it out on the companion-hatch, we again, for the third or fourth time, gave a careful look at it.

"I cannot understand the set of this current," he said. "It probably sweeps round the island. But we are being carried much closer than I like to be in so perfect a calm. If we get a breeze it will be all right, but—"

Just then the sails gave several loud flaps, as if some one had shaken them out, and the schooner rolled now to one side, now to the other. Her head had moved so as to bring the swell abeam. Once having begun, she went on making the same unpleasant movements. It was evident that the swell had increased.

"Is there no way to stop her from doing that?" asked Mary.

"Not till the wind fills her sails," answered Harry. "I hope, however, that we shall get a breeze before long."

Harry did not say this in a very cheerful tone. He soon afterwards beckoned Tom Platt to him, and I saw them talking earnestly together for some minutes. I joined them. They were discussing the probable set of the current, which was at present sweeping us at the rate of at least three knots an hour towards the reef.

"We might keep her off it, at all events, until a breeze springs up," remarked Tom.

"We'll have the boats out, then, and do our best," said my brother, and he gave the order "Out boats."

We carried two boats on the davits, but as they were too light to be of much service, we hoisted out the long-boat, which was stowed amidships. We also lowered one of the gigs. The two boats were at once made fast to the tow-line. The men gave way, and the schooner's head was kept off from the threatening reef, against which the sea was breaking with tremendous force. The men bent to their oars, for they knew the danger as well as we did.

We all watched the reef with anxious eyes. Should the vessel be driven against it, we should, in a few seconds, we well knew, be dashed to pieces; and, though we might escape in the boats before that catastrophe occurred, we should be left to make a long voyage before we could reach any civilised people. All around us were islands, most of them, we had reason to fear, inhabited by treacherous and blood-thirsty savages.

We, of course, did not express our anxiety to the ladies, who, however, I thought, began to suspect that the vessel was in danger, although they said nothing. The men had been pulling fully an hour against the current, and yet, as I looked at the reef, I could not help acknowledging to myself that the vessel was nearer than at first. The swell, at the same time, began to increase, and we could now hear the roar of the breakers as they dashed against the wall of coral which interrupted their progress.

"We'll send the other boat ahead, Platt," said my brother.

"Ay, ay, sir," answered Tom; and he and I with the two remaining men lowered her, and, jumping in, joined our shipmates in towing, leaving only my brother with Dick and Nat to take charge of the vessel. He now ordered us to pull across the current, in the hopes of thus in time getting out of it. We all pulled away with a will, making the schooner move faster through the water than she had done for many hours.

"We must manage it somehow," shouted Tom to the other boats. "Give way, lads—give way. We shall soon be clear of the current."

It was of little use urging the men, as they were already straining every nerve. My brother walked the deck, stopping every now and then, casting his eyes frequently around the horizon in the hopes of discovering signs of a coming breeze. Then he would look towards the reef, but there was nothing encouraging to be seen in that direction. Still Tom shouted every now and then, "Pull away, lads—pull away!"

"We are pulling, mate, as hard as we can," answered the men from the other boats.

If we had any doubts of it before it was now clear enough that an unusually strong current was setting us towards the reef, even faster than we could pull away from it. Whenever the men showed any signs of relaxing their efforts Harry came to the bows and cheered them on, leaving Dick to steer. It was somewhat trying work for all of us, for the hot sun was beating down on our heads, the perspiration streaming from every pore; but our lives depended upon our exertions, and pull we must to the last moment. I heard some of the men talking of going alongside the schooner and asking the captain for a glass of grog apiece.

"Don't be thinking of that, lads," cried Tom. "It would be so much precious time lost. We can pull well enough if we have the will. The grog would not give you any real strength, and you'd be as thirsty as before a few minutes afterwards. Can't one of you strike up a tune, and see if that don't help us along."

There was no response to this appeal, so Tom himself at once began shouting a no very melodious ditty. First one man joined in, then another and another, until the whole of the boats' crews were singing at the top of their voices. It appeared to me that the vessel was moving somewhat faster than before through the water, but looking towards the wall of foam that seemed no further off. Still we knew that our efforts were of use, as we thus considerably delayed the destruction which awaited our vessel should she once get within the power of the breakers. Hour after hour passed by. The swell had increased, and, combined with the current, made our task still more difficult, but Harry had too much at stake to let any consideration for our fatigue induce him to allow us to rest for a moment. "Pull on, lads, pull on," he shouted. "We shall have the breeze before long, and we'll not let the schooner be cast away."

The roar of the breakers sounded in our ears between each dip of the oars. I looked round, but no sign of a breeze could I discover. My heart sank within me as I thought of how Harry must be *feeling* with the dear ones under his charge in so great a peril. As I again looked towards the reef it seemed that, since we could not tow the vessel off, no power could save her. I knew that the depth of water close up to these coral reefs is generally so great that there would not be a possibility of anchoring, nor did I see any opening through which we could pass and get into smooth water.

At last Harry shouted out, "Mr Platt, in the second gig, come alongside and help trim sails." We at once obeyed him.

"What do you think we shall get out of that, Platt," he asked, pointing to a small cloud which was seen rising above the horizon.

"A stiffish breeze, to my mind, and I hope we shall get it before long," answered Tom.

We at once trimmed sails, and while we were so employed I saw several cats'-paws playing over the surface. The sails filled.

"Let the boats come alongside, and we'll hoist them in before the breeze catches us," cried Harry. "We shall do now, without their help, I hope."

This was speedily done, but scarcely had we secured the larger boat, the first gig having already been hoisted on board, than the wind filling our canvas, the vessel heeled over almost to her gunwale. But the danger was not past, we had still that fearful wall of surf under our lee. It would be no easy matter to beat off it.

The awning had been quickly unrigged, and the schooner, with as much canvas as she could bear, was tearing through the fast rising seas. We stood on, still nearing the reef. Old Tom went to the helm. The wind increasing, the vessel heeled over before it, but it would not do to shorten sail. The men were at their stations.

"We'll go about, Platt, and see if she'll do better on the other tack," said Harry. "Helm's a lee!" About she came, but scarcely had she gathered way when a more furious blast than before laid her over. I looked aloft—the top masts were bending like willow wands. I feared every instant that they would go, but it was not a moment to shorten sail. Presently the wind headed us, and we had once more to go about. We now stood on almost parallel with the reef, Tom watching for every slight variation of the wind to edge the schooner off it. All this time, though the current no longer carried us towards the reef, the heavy swell rolling in threatened to set us on it. Night was approaching. It would add greatly to the danger of our position. The ladies had hitherto remained on deck, fully aware of our peril, but showing no signs of fear. Harry, who from the moment the gale sprang up had stood holding on to the weather backstay, now watching the canvas, now the fast rising seas, urged them and Nat to go below.

"I will summon you, if necessary," he said, in a calm tone. "But we will hope for the best. Remain in the cabin, and keep your cloaks and hats ready to put on."

They went without remonstrance. I helped them down the companion-ladder.

"Is there much danger, do you think, Ned?" asked Mary.

"Harry seems unusually grave."

"We must, as he says, hope for the best," I answered, though I myself knew that the danger was imminent. Should a spar go or the gale increase, there would be but scant time, before the schooner would be among the breakers, to get into the boats; and even should we escape in them, would they live in that stormy sea? I saw Mary and Fanny kneel down at the sofa as I left the cabin, and Mary drawing Nat to her side.

"Their prayers will help us," I thought, as I sprang on deck.

The wind was increasing, the foam-topped seas rolled in quick succession towards us, the sky to windward looked threatening in the extreme; that terrible wall of foam loomed higher through the gloom of night. Still, as long as the schooner's head could be kept turned away from the reef, we might hope to claw off from it. The chart had shown us that a reef existed, but its form was indistinctly marked. Hitherto we had found it running in a direct line, north and south, but it might suddenly trend to the east, and if so, without a moment's warning, we might be upon it. Harry, knowing this, had stationed two of the men with the sharpest sight forward, to look out for breakers ahead, that should they be seen, we might go about and have a chance of escaping them; but, owing to the heavy sea rolling in, there was a great risk of the schooner missing stays, and should she do so, our fate would be sealed: there, would be no time to get the boats out before she would be among the breakers. Harry now told me to go forward to assist the other men on the look-out.

"We'll not go about, if we can help it," he said. "The water is deep close up to the reef, and a miss is as good as a mile."

Not a word was spoken; the crew were at their stations ready

W. H. G. Kingston

to execute the orders they might receive. The increased roar of the ceaseless breakers showed me that we were nearer than hitherto, though the vessel was tearing along through the seas at her fastest speed, taking the water over the bows in dense showers which often prevented me from seeing ahead.

"Shall we never get to the end of this terrible reef?" I said to myself. Just then I saw close on the starboard bow the snowy wall of surf. "Luff! Luff all you can!" I shouted out, my cry being echoed by the men. The next moment we appeared to be in the very midst of the seething waters, which fell foaming down on our deck. I gave up all for lost, but again the schooner dashed on and we were free. The reef was yet, however, on our starboard side, but as I peered through the darkness I observed a gap in the wall of foam. I ran aft to Harry. He had seen it.

"We must venture through," he said. "Square away the fore-yard. Ease off the main-sheet; up with the helm."

His orders were obeyed, while he hurried aft to direct Tom how to steer. The hissing breakers rose on either hand not twenty fathoms from the vessel; the seas roared up astern; now a huge billow lifted us, and then down we glided into comparatively smooth water.

"Stand by to shorten sail!" shouted Harry. "Port the helm!"

"Port it is," cried Tom.

The headsails were handed, the schooner was rounded to, the anchor let go, and she rode in safety inside the reef. Harry, with a light heart, sprang below to assure his wife and her sister that the danger was past. We could but dimly make out the low shore on the other side of the lagoon; but what was the character of the island, or whether or not it was inhabited, we could not tell. The wind was still blowing with great force, the breakers dashing with terrific roars against the reef outside of us, so that at any moment we might be driven from our anchor. We both of us therefore intended to stay on deck during the remainder of the night, to be ready should any accident occur. We, however, went down to supper, for which we were very ready, as we had eaten nothing since the commencement of the gale. Very pleasant the cabin looked after the gloomy deck, with Mary and Fanny seated at the table, and the swinging lamp shedding a bright light around. It was difficult to believe that not many minutes before there was a fearful prospect of our vessel being dashed to pieces on the rocks. We could, however, remain below but a very short time, and had again to hurry on deck.

"I'm afraid she's dragging her anchor, sir," said Tom, who was getting a lead line ready to ascertain whether this was the case.

The lead was dropped to the bottom, the line ran out slowly, showing that his surmise was correct. More cable was paid out in the hope of bringing her up. We looked anxiously astern, fearing that she might strike on some mass of coral between us and the shore. At length, to our great relief, the line hung up and down, showing that the anchor was holding. The night passed slowly on. Seldom have I more anxiously wished for the return of day.

CHAPTER THREE

Daylight showed us that the reef, through an opening in which we had passed, was many miles in circumference, and that it surrounded several islands of various sizes and heights, with cocoanut, pandanus, and a few other trees and shrubs growing on them. They were not, as we had at first supposed, lagoon islands. Harry said that he believed them to be the summits of the hills of a submerged island, of which the reef marked the outer edge. We inspected the nearest through our glasses, but could not discover any signs of inhabitants, not a hut, not a canoe on the beach, not a wreath of smoke ascending beyond the trees. In the distance, as if floating on the calm surface of the water, appeared, blue and indistinct, the other islands of the group, one of the most northern of which we had seen on the previous day. The gale had ceased, though the breakers still dashed furiously on the outer side of the reef, but scarcely a ripple disturbed the placid expanse of the lagoon.

"Oh, how beautiful!" exclaimed Fanny, as she and Mary came on deck. "I should so like to take a stroll through that shady grove on the soft turf which carpets the ground."

"Do let us go, Harry," said Mary; "you are not obliged to sail immediately."

Nat also begged that he might go.

"While the swell rolls in through the passage with this light breeze we cannot safely attempt to get out, and so, as you wish it, we will pay a visit to the nearest island," answered Harry. "But I warn you that you may be disappointed."

As soon as we had breakfasted the two gigs were lowered. Harry took the two ladies in one, and I had charge of the other, having with me Nat and Dick Tilston. Just as we were about to shove off I asked Tom to hand me down Harry's fowling-piece, on the chance of getting a shot at some birds.

"May as well have a musket, too," he said, giving me one with some ammunition. "There may be no people ashore, or if there are they may be friendly, but it's as well to be prepared for t'other in these parts."

Tom seldom indulged in so long a speech. It showed that he was somewhat anxious about our going on shore on an unknown island. We gave way, eager to step on shore, my boat soon catching up Harry's. As we approached the beach we found that the surf washing over the outer reef set upon it in a way which would have made landing there disagreeable, so we pulled a short distance round to the lee side, where we discovered a little bay, or indentation in the coral rock, large enough to admit both the boats, I getting in first was in readiness to hand Mary and Fanny on shore.

"Why, what has become of the soft green turf we saw?" exclaimed Fanny, looking along under the trees.

"Perhaps we shall find it further on," remarked Mary.

"I am afraid not," said Harry; "but we will go on through the shady groves and try to reach it."

It was no easy matter to do this, for although there was grass, it grew in wiry patches out of the coral rock, in some places so thickly that we were compelled to wind in and out among them to make any progress. No flowers nor fruits were to be seen, except some cocoanuts high up above our heads, while the sun came down between the scanty foliage with no less force than on the water. Still our curiosity tempted us to proceed, but everywhere was the same wiry grass which we had taken at a distance for soft turf. At length we came to an open space, raised but slightly above the level of the sea. It was tenanted by innumerable aquatic birds—gannets, sooty terns, beautiful tropic and frigate birds, the nests of the latter constructed of rough sticks covering the boughs of the surrounding trees. While the gannets, whose eggs had been deposited on the ground without nests refused to move as we approached— only exhibiting their alarm or displeasure by loud croaks, and allowing us to catch hold of them without resistance—the frigate birds, more wary, rose from their perches, inflating their blood-red pouches to the size of large cocoanuts, as they ascended high up in the air above our heads, or flew off to sea; others circled round us screeching wildly and flapping their wings. The discordant noise, the heat, the disagreeable smell, and the roughness of the ground, made the ladies unwilling to proceed further, and they proposed returning slowly to the boats; but Dick, Nat, and I, with Jack Lizard, one of the men, pushed forward in spite of all obstacles, as I was anxious to explore more of the island.

"Do not be long away," shouted Harry; "we may have a breeze shortly, and must get aboard."

"Ay, ay!" I answered, as we hurried on, expecting to be able to get to the other side of the island and to turn back and overtake them before they reached the boats. The ground rose slightly as we advanced, showing that the island had been upheaved, since first formed by its minute architects, owing to some volcanic convulsion far down in the depths of the ocean. Masses of coral worn by time lay scattered about, amid which grew shrubs and tangled creepers, with here and there a few taller trees; but as the shrubs were not of a thorny species we pushed through them or leaped over them, Dick and Nat coming down on their noses more than once in our progress. Seeing a knoll, or rather a mass of coral, thrown up higher than the rest ahead I made for it, hoping to get from thence a more extensive view than we could from where we were. We soon climbed to the summit, which was high enough to enable us to look over the surrounding trees.

"Hillo, what are those dots out there?" exclaimed Nat, pointing towards the eastern end of the nearest island, which we had seen from the schooner.

"Dots, do you call them, young gentleman?" said Lizard; "to my mind they are canoes, well-nigh a score of them; and they are making way over the water at a pretty fast rate, too, towards us." I had not brought a telescope, but shading my eyes with my hands the better to examine the objects I was satisfied that Lizard was right, and that they were canoes. At first I did not suppose that they, or rather the people in them, had any hostile intentions; but suddenly the idea occurred to me that they had discovered the schooner, and were coming with the design of cutting her off. Should such be the case, it was important to warn my brother without delay, that we might return on board and prepare for the defence of the vessel.

"More nor likely, Mr Ned," answered Lizard when I asked him his opinion. "As the mate was a saying afore we came away, you can never trust those black fellows."

"Come on, boys, then," I cried. "We must make good use of

our legs, or the canoes will be up to us before we can reach the boats."

We set off, keeping close together that we might help each other in case of any of us being hurt by falling. First Dick came down, and then Nat had two tumbles, both scratching their hands and knees; but, the moment they were on their feet, on they came again. I got an ugly fall, which would have been much worse if Lizard had not caught me, and, as it was, I cut one of my knees and hands on the sharp coral. At length we had to stop and take breath, for, having not only to run, but often to leap from rock to rock, it was very exhausting work.

"Are we going the right way?" asked Nat, looking round.

It was well he asked the question, for, on climbing a short way up a tree, I discovered that we had been keeping too much to the right, and should have arrived at the east instead of at the south side of the island, where we had landed. Correcting our mistake, we again went on, and I was very thankful when we came to the level part inhabited by the colony of birds. We dashed through them, crushing many an egg, as well as several hapless young ones, regardless of the screechings of the old birds and the furious pecks they gave at our legs. I looked out ahead, but could see nothing of Harry and the ladies. We shouted, thinking that they might not be far off; but, receiving no answer, I hoped that they had already embarked.

At last I caught sight of Harry, with Mary and Fanny seated near him, both with their sketch-books before them. At that moment a gun was fired from the schooner.

"Why, what's the matter?" exclaimed Harry.

Scarcely had he asked the question than another gun was fired.

"Old Tom thinks there's danger somewhere, and wants us aboard again."

I was unwilling to alarm Mary and Fanny, so, instead of shouting out, I waited till I could get up to my brother, when I told him quietly what we had seen.

"The sooner we are aboard the better, for the canoes appear to be coming on at a great rate," I added.

"No doubt about it," he answered; and, telling the ladies to shut up their books, he hurried with them towards the boats, bidding Lizard and Dick to run on ahead and order the men to be in readiness to shove off. We were not long in reaching the boats, and we prepared to return in the order we had left the schooner, I having Dick and Nat with me. Harry's boat got off first, and his crew gave way with a will; mine followed at some little distance. Just as we opened the eastern point of the island I got sight of the fleet of canoes coming round it, and steering directly for the schooner. Old Tom saw us coming, yet he fired again, probably in the hopes of scaring the natives and preventing them from attacking us; but this did not appear to have any effect on them, perhaps because they were ignorant of the power of firearms. Fast as we were pulling they came along faster, and it seemed doubtful if we should reach the schooner before they were up to us. As yet they were some way to the eastward, so that the course on which they were approaching the schooner formed an angle of about thirty degrees with that on which we were steering; thus, a shot fired from her, might hit them without the risk of injuring us. We had come away with only three hands in the boat besides Dick. I made him take the stroke-oar, that I might assist him, while I

W. H. G. Kingston

placed Nat at the helm. I now told Nat to edge up slightly to the eastward, so that we might keep between Harry's boat and the savages. Though we bent to our oars, the canoes were gaining on us. It was just possible that their intentions were friendly, but it would be folly to trust to them. How I wished for a breeze, that the schooner might get under weigh and come to our assistance! There was, however, not a breath of wind to fill her sails, so that we must, I saw, depend on our own exertions. Old Tom did not again fire, probably because he considered that, unless he could hit one of the canoes, the savages would fancy that the shot would do them no harm. The canoes were now so near that I could distinguish their character. Though small compared with those of Fiji and Tonga, the leading ones were double, with a platform in the centre, on which stood a number of men gesticulating violently, and flourishing spears and clubs, while others sat on either side working broad-bladed paddles almost upright at a rapid rate. I could have picked off some of the warriors, but was unwilling to commence hostilities. I looked round, and was thankful to see that Harry's boat was getting near the schooner. In a few minutes he and his companions would be on board. Before then, however, my boat would be on a line with the canoes, and a shot fired from the vessel might strike her. Just as this idea occurred to me there came a flash and a loud report, and as I looked astern to see the effect produced by the shot, I saw that the canoes were thrown into considerable confusion. The leading one had been struck, and the platform knocked to pieces. The warriors were tumbling overboard, while the other canoes, coming up, were running into the wreck and into each other. Whether any one had been killed I could not see. Dick and the rest of my crew shouted as they saw what had happened.

"Give way, lads, give way," I cried out. "We may get on board now and defend the vessel, if the savages venture to attack us."

We had got almost up to the schooner, and Harry had put the ladies on board her before the savages had recovered from their alarm, the warriors and crew of the wreck having got on board the other canoes. Notwithstanding the effect of Tom's shot, they seemed bent on attacking us, and once more came paddling on.

"We must show the savages that we are not afraid of them," cried Harry, turning his boat's head towards the canoes, and standing up with a musket in his hand. He had obtained two from the vessel. I imitated his example, and all hands raised a loud, ringing cheer, which no sooner did the savages hear than they ceased paddling, and when we, firing our muskets, dashed forward, they fairly turned tail, or rather backing away, went off in all directions. A few more musket shots fired over their heads increased their speed.

"I told you, Mr Ned, that you'd find the small arms of use," said Tom, when we got on board. "They ain't accustomed to big guns, and don't know what a round shot can do."

"It was your round shot, however, which stopped them when they were nearly up with us; and I hope that they won't forget the lesson they have learned to-day," I answered. I need not say that Mary and Fanny looked very thankful when they saw us safe on board.

We anxiously watched the savages, for we could not be certain of their intentions. They might rally and renew the attack, if not in the daytime, during the night, when we should be unable to see them till they were close upon us. Our hope therefore was that the wind would again spring up, and that we should be able to get to sea before darkness set in. In vain, however, we waited for a breeze. The canoes meantime had disappeared behind the nearest island; but we could not ascertain whether they had gone on to the further-

W. H. G. Kingston

off islands or were still in our neighbourhood. In the latter case they might come suddenly upon us, and it would be necessary to keep a very watchful look-out to avoid being taken by surprise. I volunteered to go on shore and ascertain where they were, by making my way through the wood across the island, till I reached some point whence I could obtain a view over the water on the north side; but Harry would not allow me to run the risk, for had I been discovered I should in all probability have been put to death. He, however, took one of the boats, and surveyed the whole of the channel through which we should have to pass to get to sea, that, should a breeze spring up during the night, we might get out without fear of running on the reef. By the time he returned on board evening was drawing on. He had directed Tom to fire a gun as a signal should the canoes appear, but not one was seen before it became so dark that we could scarcely distinguish the outline even of the nearest island. Mary and Fanny having recovered from their alarm, for they had naturally been much frightened, were seated in the well-lighted cabin, with Nat, at tea, when Harry and I joined them. We had left old Tom and Dick in charge of the watch on deck, consisting of Tom Tubb the New Zealander, and Jacky Pott the Sandwich Islander, with two other men. The guns were loaded, the muskets arranged against the companion-hatch, and the cable was hove short, so that we might speedily trip the anchor and make sail should the wished-for breeze spring up. We almost forgot, as we were enjoying our comfortable meal in our cozy cabin, that not far off were hordes of howling savages; that we had to find our way between coral reefs, and might have storms and other unknown dangers to encounter. Tea over, after singing a few airs to the accompaniment of her guitar, Fanny took up her work, while Mary as usual began to read. I then went on deck.

"Any chance of a breeze soon?" I asked.

"Not a breath of wind as yet, sir," answered old Tom; "and I don't think we shall get it till the morning. I only hope when it does come that we shan't have more of it than we want. I'd advise the ladies not to sit up till we are out at sea, for if they do they'll get but little sleep to-night."

I went below and told them what Tom said. Harry agreed that he was right; and when they retired to their cabins he and I returned on deck. We neither of us felt inclined to turn in. Perhaps we were as anxious as if we had been certain that the savages would attack us. The hours, as they always do on such occasions, went slowly by; and at last, unable longer to keep my eyes open, I got a cloak from below, and rolling myself up in it lay down on deck. How long I had slept I could not tell, when I heard Tom exclaim—

"I see them, sir."

"You are right; so do I," answered Harry. "Turn the hands up."

I was on my feet in an instant, and looking towards the eastern end of the island distinctly made out a number of dark objects on the surface of the water approaching the schooner. The men came tumbling up on deck.

"Silence!" cried Harry, in a low voice; "crouch down so as not to show yourselves. As the savages hope to surprise us, we must surprise them. Ned, run down and tell Mary and Fanny that we may have to fire the guns, but that they must not be alarmed, as we are sure to beat off the savages."

I quickly executed my commission, and sprang again on deck. The canoes did not appear to me to have got nearer. The savages were, perhaps, holding a consultation. As I was looking at them, I felt a breath of air on my right cheek. It

W. H. G. Kingston

was from the eastward. Again it came stronger. It was the most favourable wind we could have.

"Loose the headsails—man the windlass," cried Harry. "I shall be thankful if we can avoid injuring more of the ignorant savages."

The anchor was quickly hove up—the headsails and then the mainsail set, and the schooner glided on towards the passage through the reef. As her broadside was turned towards the canoes we could fire all our guns at them, should it be necessary. Almost immediately afterwards the moon rose, showing us clearly their position, and, what was of more consequence, enabling us with less difficulty to see our way through the passage. The canoes now came paddling on, the savages probably fearing that we should escape them.

"We must not let them attack us in the channel," said Harry, and he reluctantly gave Tom the order to fire. Our guns were discharged in quick succession, and the next instant we saw the canoes paddling away in the utmost confusion; but it was too dark to ascertain what injury had been inflicted. We had soon to haul aft the sheets, and to devote all our attention to the navigation of our vessel—old Tom going forward to look out for dangers, and Harry standing aft to direct the helmsman and conn the vessel, while the crew were at their stations; I standing by the main-sheet with others to flatten it aft or ease it off as might be necessary. Now and then I took a look astern to ascertain if the canoes were following us, but could only just make them out, showing that the savages had had enough of it, though they might have annoyed us greatly had they boldly attacked us while we were standing through the passage. In a short time the outer part of the reef was passed, and the breeze freshening we were gliding swiftly over the moonlit sea.

CHAPTER FOUR

When morning broke, the reef-encircled islands could be indistinctly seen over the port-quarter rising out of the sparkling ocean. The wind being against us we expected to have a long beat before we could reach our destination; but Harry resolved to persevere, hoping that we might get a favourable breeze at last. Things on board went on as usual. After I had had my sleep out in the forenoon I gave Dick a lesson in navigation, which I had done regularly every day of late since I discovered that he was anxious to learn.

"I am most grateful to you, Mr Ned," he said. "If I can fit myself to be an officer I shall not be ashamed to return home, which I should have had I gained no more knowledge than I should have done under ordinary circumstances, as a ship's boy."

"Much depends on the way you work, and whether you keep to your good resolutions," I observed. "But I say, Dick, you have never told me anything about yourself; though from the first I saw that you had had a good education."

"To tell you the truth, my father is a merchant in London, and my mother moves in good society," he answered, speaking rapidly. "She was very fond of me, and I do not think that if I had been with her I could have run away; but I went off from school, where I was not happy, quite forgetting how miserable it would make her when she heard that I was missing. The thought of that has preyed on my mind more than anything else. I wrote to her, however, when I reached Brisbane, and paid the postage with the last shilling I had, so that she knows now that I am alive, though I did not like to tell her how miserable I was. I only asked her and my father to forgive me, and promised to return home when I had made my fortune, for I just then fancied if I could escape from the ship that I should be able to do that. I soon found when I did get on shore that I was miserably mistaken, and if it had not been for you I believe that I should have died. I am sure that none of my own brothers, of whom I have five older than I am, could have treated me more kindly. I have three sisters also, and when I look at Mrs Morton and Miss Fanny they remind me of them, and I think of my folly in leaving them all and running the chance of never seeing them again."

After Dick had made this confession I felt more than ever inclined to befriend him.

When I told Harry, he said that he would consider what was right to be done. "I think it best, however, that Dick should remain in his present position for a time," he added. "He is learning the details of seamanship from old Tom and the rudiments of navigation from you, and as he does not mix much with the crew he will gain no harm from them."

We were standing on that evening close hauled to the south-east when, just as the sun went down, dark clouds began to gather to windward.

"We'll shorten sail at once," said Harry. "It may not come on to blow, but it looks like it and we cannot be too cautious." He issued the order to Tom, and we soon had the schooner under snug canvas. It was fortunate that she was. Not ten minutes afterwards, just as Harry had gone below, a squall struck her.

"Luff! Luff!" shouted Tom, but before Jack Lizard, who was at the helm, could do so, over the schooner heeled, till the water rushed through the scuppers high up her deck. Lower and lower she went, until I thought she was going to capsize. Harry sprang up from below. Tom had rushed forward, and with the hands stationed there let fly the jib-sheets, and was hauling down the forestay-sail—the foresail had been stowed. Suddenly she rose, and I heard a loud crack, like the report of a musket fired close to my ear.

"We've sprung the mainmast, I fear," exclaimed Harry, and he called the men aft to lower the mainsail, while he and I sprang to the peak and throat halliards to let them go. On examining the mast we found that it was so badly sprung that it would be impossible again to set sail on it without the risk of carrying it away. It seemed a wonder that it had not gone altogether.

"We must bear up for Samoa," said Harry. "It is very provoking, but there is no place nearer where we can hope to obtain a fresh spar."

Accordingly the headsails were again hoisted, the fore-topsail was set, and the helm being put up, away we ran before the wind on a course for Upalu, the centre island of the group, in which Apia, the chief port, is situated. The wind increased, and we soon had to close-reef the fore-topsail, the only sail we could carry; then down came the rain in huge drops, or rather in sheets which wetted us as thoroughly as if we had jumped overboard, and so deluged the deck that had it not run out at the scuppers as the vessel rolled from side to side the water would have been up to our

W. H. G. Kingston

ankles in a few minutes. What with the pattering of the rain, the howling of the wind and the dashing of the sea, we could scarcely hear each other's voices. Though we had no sail set on the mainmast, and had secured it with spars lashed round the injured part, and additional stays, I frequently, as the schooner pitched into the fast rising seas, expected to see it carried away altogether. Old Tom, who seemed to have the same fear, told us to look out and stand from under, in case it should go, but the difficulty was to know in what direction it would fall, should it come down.

On we ran day after day, the gale apparently following us, though Harry said that as storms were generally circular we should in time run out of it. Each time, however, that I turned out to keep my watch, there we were, running on; the seas leaping and hissing and foaming around us; the dark clouds flying overhead; the vessel rolling and pitching in the same uncomfortable fashion as before. Harry did his best to keep up the spirits of his wife and Fanny, who behaved like heroines, though they agreed that they little expected to meet with such weather in the Pacific.

"It is as well to get it over, and we may hope to have finer for the rest of the voyage," answered Harry, to console them.

We had other dangers to encounter, of which he did not speak. Although the sea we were traversing was pretty well known by this time, there might be small islands or coral reefs improperly placed on the chart, or not laid down at all, and at any moment during the darkness of night, or even in the daytime, we might come upon one, when in an instant the vessel would have been dashed to pieces, and all on board must have perished. We had, therefore, to keep the sharpest possible look-out, for a moment's want of vigilance might cause our destruction. Once I saw the sea leaping and foaming high up above the surrounding water away on the starboard hand. I pointed out the spot to Tom.

"The end of a reef," he observed. "If we'd been a little more to the nor'ard we should likely enough have been on it, but a miss is as good as a mile. We may be thankful to have escaped."

He afterwards told me that we passed another reef to the northward while I was below, how many we escaped during the night we could not tell. Thus some of the dangers to be encountered by those navigating among coral islands will be understood. At length, one morning when I came on deck to keep my watch, I saw the stars shining brightly overhead— the wind had fallen, the sea was going down, and the schooner, with her squaresail rigged out, was running gaily along. At noon we took an observation, when we found that we were less than a hundred miles from the port of Apia, which we therefore expected to reach the next day, unless the wind should fail us.

We were more fortunate than we expected. Early the next morning the land was seen over the port bow rising in a succession of ridges to a moderate height above the sea. We had made an excellent landfall, for the harbour of Apia was almost directly ahead. Before we reached it, a large whaleboat came off and put an Englishman on board, who introduced himself as the chief pilot of the place. He carried us through a somewhat intricate passage between coral rocks to a safe anchorage not far from the shore.

We were surprised to see several tastefully-built houses among trees, a large church, stores, and other buildings, besides a number of whitewashed cottages, many of which, the pilot told us, were inhabited by natives who have learned the art of building and the use of lime from the missionaries. Through their instrumentality also, although but a few years

W. H. G. Kingston

ago the people inhabiting different parts of the island were constantly fighting with each other, warfare has entirely ceased, and all have become Christians by profession, many of them adorning the Gospel by their lives and conversation, while others have gone forth to carry its blessings to the still benighted heathen in the western islands of the Pacific.

I must be brief in my account of the events which occurred during our stay at Apia. On going on shore we were received with great kindness by several of the English and American residents, who invited Harry and his wife and her sister to take up their abode at their houses, but they preferred sleeping on board the schooner. We were fortunate in finding a mast from a vessel wrecked on the coast, which by cutting down slightly could be made to replace the mainmast we had sprung.

We had been in harbour a couple of days when a fine-looking young chief came on board, prompted by curiosity to see the vessel so unlike the whalers which generally visit the port. He was unpicturesquely dressed in shirt and trousers and we should not have taken him to be a chief, except from his handsome figure, unless he had introduced himself as Toa, the nephew of the great chief Maleatoa. He spoke English well, and seemed very intelligent. On being introduced to Mary and Fanny, he made a bow which would have become a French courtier, and appeared wonderfully struck by them. He soon drew me aside and inquired who they were. When I told him that one was married to my brother, and the other was her sister, he appeared suddenly lost in thought, but said nothing at the time. We asked him into the cabin, as we were just going to sit down to dinner. He behaved in all respects like a polished gentleman, narrowly watching us, and imitating the way he saw us eat. He told us a great deal about his country, the progress it had made during the last few years since the inhabitants had become Christians and wars had ceased; the roads that had been constructed, the houses built, the fields cultivated, and horses and cattle introduced. He described their astonishment on first seeing a large animal, a mule, which they supposed to be an enormous dog, and accordingly gave it an appropriate name. In return for the civility we had shown him on board, he invited me to accompany him on a sporting expedition into the interior.

"I will show you how we catch pigeons and kill wild hogs," he said.

Harry gave me leave to go, and I asked if Dick might accompany me, as I knew he would like it. My brother consented. On going on shore early the next morning we found the chief and several companions waiting for us. Each person carried a tame pigeon on his arm secured by a string, as also a bamboo thirty or forty feet long with a small net at the end of it. Several attendants accompanied us carrying guns and ammunition.

"We shall depend upon the provisions we find in the woods for our support," said Toa to me. "We can easily obtain all we require."

We proceeded for about four hours amid tangled bushes, across marshes, and up the slippery sides of hills, till we arrived at a district with here and there open spots, but generally covered with brushwood. The attendants set to work to clear away a large circle by cutting down the brushwood; we then retired to a spot which had been previously fixed on, where a camp was formed, and some, arbours which would shelter us for the night erected. Some of our people had in the meantime collected some wild bread-fruit, dug up some wild yams, and brought down some cocoanuts, which gave us an ample repast. Formerly the

W. H. G. Kingston

chiefs would have indulged in drinking kava, but that custom had been abandoned. Having satisfied our hunger we returned to our ambushes round the ring. Each sportsman, if so he could be called, now stuck a stick with a cross-piece on it into the ground for his pigeon, which was secured by a string forty yards in length, to perch on. After remaining a short time quiet Toa gave the signal, and the birds were simultaneously thrown into the air, when they flew up and commenced, as they had been taught, wheeling round and round. In a short time a number of wild pigeons seeing them from a distance, and supposing from their movements that they were hovering over their food, came from all directions to join them. I was much surprised at the dexterity with which as the wild birds circled among the decoy pigeons the sportsmen, rapidly raising their nets, captured them. The moment a bird was caught the net was again raised and another captured in the same manner. Toa in this way caught a dozen in as many minutes. Dick and I tried our skill, but we only knocked against the tame birds. It was a long time before I managed to catch even one; Dick was still less successful. It seemed at first very easy, but then it must be remembered that the rods were upwards of thirty feet long, and that the birds flew very rapidly. "Formerly," said Toa to us, "large parties of young men used to go out for a month together, but we have now other occupation for our time, and only now and then engage in the sport."

"This is a funny sort of fishing in the air," said Dick.

"I call it birding," I answered.

"Very right," observed Toa; "I will show you how we fish some day."

We caught several dozen pigeons during the morning. The afternoon was to be devoted to hog-shooting, at a spot a short distance off. We were divided into two parties—Dick and I accompanied Toa, while another young chief, who had arrived with a number of ugly-looking dogs, led another party.

After going some distance we arrived at a spot where the pigs had been rooting about, and away went the curs in chase. Before long their shrill yelping bark told us that the herd was found, and following the sound we discovered the chief and a companion tying the legs of a young boar, which had been caught by running it down with some of the dogs. The barking increased as we went on.

Presently Toa cried out, "Take care; get behind the trees all of you," and we saw an enormous wild boar which the dogs had been keeping at bay.

The chief advanced running from tree to tree with great rapidity, that he might get near enough to the animal to shoot it without injuring the dogs. At length the boar caught sight of him and charged. Toa fired, and apparently missed, and the brute came rushing towards me. I aimed at his fore-shoulder, hoping, if I did not kill him outright, to stop his career. In another moment he would have been into my side, for I had no time to reload, when, just as he was near me, I made a spring and caught the bough of a tree, which I could not under other circumstances have reached, and my feet struck his back as he dashed under them. Toa had now reloaded, but before he could fire the boar again charged; he, however, nimbly sprang behind a tree, and the brute rushed past, giving me an opportunity to recover my rifle. He now caught sight of Dick, at whom he made a dash. Dick not attempting to fire, nimbly sprang up a young tree. On seeing its enemy thus escaping, the boar made a dash at the tree, and attacked it with its tusks, biting at it with the greatest fury, till Toa, approaching, settled it with a ball through its

W. H. G. Kingston

head. In this way, in a short time, we killed four large hogs, each weighing at least five hundredweight. Thus it will be seen that the sport, if exciting, was not wanting in danger, and I must own that I was very glad when it was over, and we had all escaped without wounds.

We had a luxurious supper on boar's flesh and wild pigeons, and roots and fruits of various descriptions, all of which had been collected in the woods, showing the abundance of food to be obtained in that favoured region.

After supper, Toa invited me to walk out with him away from the rest, when he confided to me his deep admiration for Fanny Amiel, and inquired whether I thought she would consent to remain at Samoa and become his wife. I did not answer at once, as I was unwilling to offend him, and yet was certain that she would not consent to any such proposal. I replied that English ladies preferred marrying their own countrymen, and then not until they were certain of their good qualities and had been long acquainted. I undertook, however, to mention the subject to my brother, but observed that I could not venture to say anything about it to the lady herself, who would be much pained at having to refuse him. He seemed somewhat downcast at my reply, but soon recovered his spirits, and we returned to the camp to prepare for sleep.

As, with the exception of wild boars, there are no savage animals in Samoa, and the people of different tribes no longer tried to surprise and murder each other, no sentries were placed, and every one laid down to rest in perfect security.

Next morning we returned to Apia. The tide was high as we went down to the harbour, at which time, when there is a swell, the breakers burst with considerable force over the reefs outside. We found a number of boys and girls swimming off, some with boards, others without them, and others paddling in paopaos, or little canoes. On reaching the reef, where the waves curled up and broke into foam, the swimmers threw themselves forward with a jump, just as the sea took them, and away they glided in the midst of the white foam, shouting and yelling at the top of their voices. The chief took us off in his canoe to see the fun. When the breaker had spent itself the swimmers were left in smooth water, on which all turned again towards the sea, breasting the smaller waves, and quietly sinking down again as the larger and stronger ones passed over, or frequently dashing boldly through them.

"They will keep at that sport till the tide falls and the reef is left bare," observed our friend Toa, as we pulled on board the schooner. "When I was a lad I was very fond of it, and could beat most of my companions, keeping longer at it and going out farther than any of them."

He had brought, I should have said, a number of pigeons and some of the wild boar's flesh as a present to Harry, and which was very acceptable on board. The ladies were on deck when we got alongside, and I was much afraid that Toa might say something to Fanny which would annoy her, before I had time to tell my brother that he might give her due warning. The young chief, however, stood in a modest manner without advancing, till Mary went up to him to thank him for his present. I in the meantime managed to tell Harry what the chief had said to me.

"I am sorry for this, but we must manage to get him on shore again as politely as possible, and I will not tell her of his proposal before he has gone."

Our attention, however, was just then attracted by seeing a

W. H. G. Kingston

vessel standing in for the harbour; she approached within a mile or so, when the wind fell. She had a signal flying for a pilot, and the men who brought us in went out to her. Toa, who had an eye to business, wishing to be on board early to see what trading could be done, said that he should go out, and invited me to accompany him in his large canoe. As we got near the vessel we found three of her boats towing ahead. On boarding her the captain said he must get in at once, as she was leaking terribly, and was besides short of provisions and water. Toa, on this, offered to bring out provisions; and the pilot told him that it was dangerous, without a leading breeze, to attempt entering the harbour, especially as the tide was falling. The brig was, I found, the *Caesar*, an American vessel, bound from California to Sydney, and had come to Apia for the reasons the captain stated.

"If you won't take her in, I will by myself," he exclaimed. "Where's the difficulty? The boats can tow her, as there isn't a breath of wind to stop her way."

"But you cannot tell how the tide will set you, and I advise you to let the boats tow you off," answered the pilot.

The skipper, however, was obstinate, and was, I suspect, pot-valiant. He ordered the boats to continue pulling ahead, while he went to the helm himself. The pilot on this, again warning him that he was risking the safety of the vessel, stepped into his boat and pulled for the harbour. Toa, however, believing that he could leave at any moment in his canoe, remained on board, and I, of course, had to stay with him. All apparently went well for some minutes, till, just as we were at the entrance, the tide caught the vessel; the after-part struck heavily; she heeled broadside on to the reef, and the next moment, with a tremendous roar, a breaker burst over us. All was confusion on board; shrieks and cries arose from the passengers, the men swearing as they rolled and slipped about. The skipper, however, recovered in a moment his self-possession, and swore he would shoot the first man that attempted to leave the vessel; but as he had no gun or revolver in his hand, no one appeared to care for the threat. One of the crew, a New Zealander, indeed, immediately jumped overboard, when the captain threw a marline-spike at his head, but, sinking, he avoided it, and managed to reach the smooth water inside the reef, where the pilot had in the meantime anchored his boat prepared to assist those who might be able to reach her. Other boats were coming off from the shore, those which had been towing, as well as the chiefs canoe, had been cut adrift directly the vessel struck, and pulled away, or they would have been swamped in an instant.

It will be understood that owing to the heavy breakers it was impossible to get off from the vessel on the sea side, and that our only hope of safety was to pass through the foaming surf on the reef, till we reached smooth water in the inside. The vessel, lightly built, was already breaking up, and her bottom planks were appearing, floating up to the surface, while the water rushed freely in and out of her. There was therefore no time to be lost. Toa at once proposed to the skipper to tie a rope to a plank, and to swim with it to the boats inside the reef, so that the passengers and those unable to help themselves might be passed along it, and their lives saved. The rope was speedily got up.

"I will go with you," I said to Toa.

"Come along," he answered, and taking my hand he jumped with me into the foaming surf. The first great roller curled high above our heads, and broke with a terrific roar. As it did so we let go the plank and sank down, keeping our eyes turned upwards to watch when it had passed. Quickly return-ing to the surface, we again clutched the plank and shoved it before us. We had twice to perform the same operation before we reached the smooth water. I wanted to return, but Toa advised me to remain, as I was not accustomed to the water as he was. He quickly again made his way along the rope to the deck of the vessel. The next moment he appeared again, holding a young lady with one arm, while he dragged himself along the rope with the other, but he twice had to descend to avoid the rollers. The young lady seemed more dead than alive when he placed her in the boat, but she quickly recovered, while he, not in the slightest degree exhausted, dashed off again on board the vessel, and brought another girl in the same way through the surf. A third time he went, and on this occasion he encountered a young man, a gentleman apparently, who was endeavouring to make his way by himself along the rope. He was clutching the rope desperately, when a roller going over him tore him away from his hold. Toa, seeing what had happened, dashed after him, and seizing him brought him back to the rope. Again Toa had to dive twice with the almost senseless stranger, whom he at length placed, greatly exhausted, in the boat. The young ladies had quickly recovered, so that I was able to pay attention to the last comer, and with the assistance of the old pilot and two other men we brought him to.

"The sooner we get ashore with these people the better, and let them have a change of duds," said the old pilot. "But I do not like leaving, while there are any people remaining on board."

"Oh, pray wait," said one of the young ladies. "There is a poor woman and her child and several other people, besides the captain and crew, who, I suppose, do not require so much help."

By this time, seeing the possibility of getting alongside the ill-fated vessel in a boat, two put off from the shore, manned by stout fellows. The first succeeded in getting alongside and bringing away a number of the passengers, but the next was less successful. The brig gave a tremendous roll, and striking the boat, capsized her in a moment, and the whole of the people were scattered about in the raging surf. They were, however, all picked up in various ways by the boats, but one poor woman had her child washed from her arms. It was being rapidly carried away by the receding sea, when Toa, who was on board the brig, sprang after it and catching it in one arm, held its head above the surf while he swam forward with the other. Thus the little fellow was borne along by his preserver. Now the brave chief rose to the summit of a foaming sea, now he sank down into the trough, again to rise with the boy still grasped in his powerful hand. In a short time he placed him in the arms of his almost frantic mother. Loud cheers burst from all the spectators as they witnessed the gallant act, which few, indeed, would have been able to accomplish.

Shortly after the last person had been taken from the brig she broke into a thousand fragments, which, with her cargo, soon, for a mile or more on either side, strewed the beach. I felt much interested in the stranger whom Toa had saved, and as he required to be attended to more than any one else, I invited him at once to come on board the *Dainty*, where I was sure Harry would be glad to receive him till he was better able than at present to go on shore. The ladies who had friends preferred at once going on shore to the house of one of the English residents. The pilot, therefore, pulled up alongside the schooner. Harry, on hearing the account I gave him, immediately begged the stranger to come on board. He signified his gratitude, but was scarcely able to speak.

As Harry and I helped him along the deck, we called old Tom and Dick to come and assist us; and with their help we carried him below.

I saw Dick looking at him with wondering eyes. At last he exclaimed—

"Who are you? Are you Charles Tilston?"

"Yes," answered the stranger, gazing at Dick's countenance; "and you are my brother Dick, whom I have come to look for."

"Yes, I am Dick," was the answer. "Oh, Charlie, I should never have forgiven myself if you had lost your life, for it was I, from what you tell me, who brought you out here."

"You will have plenty of time to talk about this by-and-by," said Harry. "Let me advise you at once to go to bed."

Charles Tilston acknowledged the wisdom of this advice, and Harry and old Tom assisting to get off his clothes put him into my berth, when having swallowed some warm broth he fell fast asleep. Dick begged that he might be allowed to remain and watch over him, promising not to speak again till he saw that his brother was sufficiently recovered to enter into conversation. As Harry thought a doctor should see our guest he sent me on shore to procure the services of one who had a short time before landed from a whaler. While I was waiting for him Toa landed, and was received with loud acclamations by all the people, the account of his having so gallantly saved the child being the theme of conversation.

As Harry was now only waiting for a breeze to sail, thinking that I might not see Toa again, I bade him farewell, and thanked him for having saved my life.

"I must come and see you to-morrow morning," he said. "You will not sail till then, as there will be no wind to carry you out. And now, my friend, I have a favour to ask, I must beg you to tell the fair Pearl of the Ocean that her figure has ever been present before my eyes, that her voice has rung in my ear, that my thoughts have been occupied with her, and her alone, ever since I saw her."

"I will not fail to deliver your message," I answered. "But I must remind you of what my brother said, and you must not be disappointed should she decline your offer." I flattered myself that I had made a very diplomatic reply, but the young chief did not look at all satisfied as I wished him good-bye.

I returned on board with the doctor, who prescribed for Charles Tilston, and said he had little doubt that he would soon come round. I did not fail to give Fanny the chiefs message. She and Mary laughed heartily.

"I must not tamper with his affections," she said, "but I cannot possibly encourage him, and I think that when he comes on board again it will be better for me not to appear."

Mary and I agreed with her, and it was settled that she should remain in the cabin when Toa paid his farewell visit. In former years had a chief conceived a similar fancy he would probably have attempted to carry off the lady by force, but this was not likely to occur under present circumstances. Harry, however, thought it prudent to keep a strong watch at night on deck. It was my middle watch, and as I was looking out across the harbour I thought I saw a fleet of canoes passing at some distance from where we lay; still, as I felt sure that Toa would not use any violence, this did not make me anxious. The canoes soon disappeared, but after some time I fancied that I again saw them hovering in the distance. Presently I heard a voice, which sounded softly as it came over the water, singing in the Samoan language. What was the meaning of the words I could not tell, but it struck me that they were those of a love ditty, and that Toa had taken this method of expressing the feelings of his heart. As Fanny was probably fast asleep in her cabin, it would be entirely thrown away upon her, and I had no intention of calling her up to listen to the serenade. I determined, however, to call Harry should the canoes approach nearer; but the song ceased, and they disappeared in the darkness.

I told old Tom, who relieved me.

"There's no harm in that sort of thing," he observed. "If the young chief takes to singing he will not dream of doing anything worse. Maybe he'll not break his heart after all, though he may think of Miss Fanny for many a long day to come."

In the morning the doctor came off again, and pronounced Charles Tilston very much better. He was able, indeed, to get up and breakfast with us in the cabin. He expressed his gratitude to Harry for the attention he had paid him, and especially for the care he had taken of Dick. He then told us, that on receiving Dick's letter he had immediately set out, by his father's desire, to bring him home. Wishing to take the shortest route, he had come over to America, and crossed the continent to San Francisco; he there found the *Caesar* on the point of sailing, and had accordingly taken a passage in her.

"I scarcely expected to reach Sydney," he said. "The skipper was drunk the greatest part of every day, and sometimes for days together. It was a mercy that we got even as far as Samoa; and had we not been wrecked, I had intended to leave the brig, and proceed by some other vessel. Now that I have found my young brother I do not like to quit him again, but I am unwilling to deprive you of his services."

"It will give me much pleasure if you will remain on board then," said Harry. Charles Tilston, greatly to my satisfaction, at once accepted the invitation; for I had taken a great fancy to him, and was unwilling also to lose Dick. Harry arranged with him to go on shore to purchase some clothing and other necessaries at the store, in case his own portmanteau should not be recovered. The natives had, in the meantime, been collecting the goods thrown upon the beach from the wrecked vessel, not one of which was stolen, and bringing them into the town. We at once went to the place where they were stowed, and among them Charles Tilston discovered his own portmanteau, which he said professed to be waterproof. On opening it, he found that no wet had got in. It being delivered to him on a small payment for salvage, we returned with it on board. All that morning the calm continued, but in the afternoon, a breeze springing up, the pilot came off, and agreed to take us out. Just as the sails were loosed, before we hove up the anchor, Toa came alongside in his canoe. As was agreed on, Fanny remained below, but Mary came on deck to receive him, and to thank him for his kindness to me, but she said nothing about her sister.

"And I am also most grateful to you for saving my life," said Charles Tilston. "Had it not been for you I am fully convinced that I should have been drowned, and I beg you to accept a few articles—all I have to offer—as a remembrance of me." On this he put into his hand a handsome clasp knife, adding some gold pieces, with which the chief seemed highly pleased. I saw him continually looking towards the companion-hatch, as if he expected Fanny to appear, but he waited in vain. At last, Harry had to remind him that we were on the point of getting under weigh, and that it would be better for him to take his leave before we hove up the anchor. He was evidently trying to say something, but his tongue seemed to cling to the roof of his mouth; and heaving a sigh he stepped into his canoe and cast off. The anchor was immediately run up to the bows, and the sails filling, as there was a leading breeze, we ran swiftly out of the harbour. I saw the young chief standing up in his canoe, and waving to us his last farewells. Not till we were well outside did Fanny venture on deck.

"Take care," said Mary laughing; "he may still come after us."

However, he did not move his paddle, and we were soon out at sea, steering with a fair breeze to the eastward.

CHAPTER FIVE

We had now a continuance of fine weather, and day after day sailed over the calm ocean, the surface just rippled by a gentle breeze, generally so much in our favour that we were able to rig out our big square sail, and to carry a topmast studding-sail. Though it was near the line the heat was not very oppressive, unless when the wind fell altogether, and then it was hot. Though I speak of the ocean being calm, there was always a perceptible swell, more perceptible when we were on the weather-side of a coral reef, against which the swell, finding an impediment to its progress, could be seen dashing with tremendous force, rising high in the air in masses of foam. We had before received a warning to keep at a respectful distance from such reefs whenever we could; but sometimes, unable to help ourselves, we were compelled to pass unpleasantly near. Night and day we kept a vigilant look-out. Sometimes, indeed, at night Harry thought it prudent to heave to, rather than attempt running on when the chart showed us that coral banks abounded ahead. In the daytime, when the sun shone, those even some way below the surface could be seen by the look-out aloft at a considerable distance, from the darker colour of the water to that of the surrounding ocean.

Though it was very delightful to have the society of Mary and Fanny, yet at other times, when danger threatened, their presence greatly increased Harry's anxieties, and I suspect that he often on these occasions wished that he had left them on shore. Mary, however, always expressed her satisfaction at being with him.

"Just think how I should have felt all the time that you were away," she said one day. "I should have been picturing you attacked by savages, or tossed about by storms, or thrown upon a coral reef, or undergoing all sorts of other misfortunes, till I got you safe back again; and I am very sure that you would not have taken as much care of yourself as you now do for my sake. So, whenever you go to sea, remember that I intend to accompany you."

We found Charles Tilston a very great addition to our society. He was well-informed, and full of life and spirits, right-minded, and earnest. He was very grateful also to Harry and me for the way we had treated Dick. He was so pleased at the account we gave of Queensland, that he proposed remaining and settling there with Dick as his companion.

We were now approaching that part of the Pacific in which Tom Platt had assured us we should find the islands round which pearl oysters abounded; but, as he could not give us the exact longitude and latitude, we expected to have to search some time before we found them. He believed it, however, to be two or three days sail to the northward of the island on which he had been cast away, and which was laid down accurately on the chart, and for that island we accordingly steered. On our course there we sighted a large lagoon island, and, as we approached the north-west end, a number of canoes came off from the shore. While at some distance the natives on board them were heard singing; as they drew near the clamour increased. Now and then they interrupted their singing by giving way to loud shouts of laughter and violent gesticulations, as if they had been a party of madmen. Their canoes were small, being only fifteen feet long, and generally containing three persons. Each canoe was furnished with an outrigger, as also with a projecting point, both over the bows and stern, to enable them to get on board out of the water. They were formed of strips of cocoanut-wood neatly sewn together. When they got within a short distance of the schooner they ceased paddling, and no signs we could make would induce them to come alongside. To calm their fears, we offered them various articles. On this one canoe paddled briskly up, near enough to have the things thrown into her; then away she went, and another approached. After this, apparently to show their gratitude, they began a monotonous song. This made us all laugh, when they stopped and grinned in return; but although they seemed inclined to be friendly, they would not trust themselves near us. Harry, however, thought that they might possibly not object to our landing on their island. A boat was accordingly lowered, and Charles Tilston, Dick, and I, with Tom Tubb, Jacky Pott, and Lizard, went in her. We carried several articles for barter, hoping, as we observed a large grove of trees on the shore, to obtain some cocoanuts. The moment the natives saw the boat, however, they paddled away and returned to the shore. As we approached the beach they assembled, shaking their spears, dancing, shouting, and making signs to us to keep off. When we retired a short distance they calmed down, but when we again approached they resumed their former behaviour, thus giving us to understand that, though they wished to be friendly, they did not desire a closer acquaintanceship. When we once more retired, they followed us in their canoes, but without exhibiting any hostility. We found that Tom Tubb, the New Zealander, could make himself clearly understood, and we desired him to say that we wanted some cocoanuts; but they replied that they had only a sufficient number for them- selves, and could not part with them. On our holding up various articles they cautiously approached, and presented us with some curious fish-hooks, matting, adzes made from the shell of the Tridachna and ground very sharp, as also with numerous pearl shells. We came to the conclusion that they had some good reason to mistrust white men; indeed, we afterwards discovered that such was the case. The articles they valued most were buttons, pieces of iron, bottles, and cloth. We tried to obtain some of their spears and clubs, but with these they would not part. As we rowed away we saw them waving green boughs, a universal sign of good-will among the Pacific islanders. Their clothing consisted of the maro, a cloth worn round the waist; the chiefs having also a mantle of matting over their shoulders, while some wore feathers in their hair. None of the females appeared; no doubt they had all been hidden as they saw us approaching. Their huts were constructed of long poles, bent so as to form a succession of arches, the ends of the poles being stuck in the ground, and the whole covered over with pandanus or palm leaves. They were evidently a very primitive race of people, and Charlie observed that if one missionary could gain their confidence he would be able to make much progress among them. Their island consisted of a coral reef of irregular shape, with a lagoon in the centre, in which were numerous knolls of various sizes rising four or five feet above the surface. The island itself, indeed, looked like a collection of islets, though in reality united by the reef, which was just a wash at half-tide, so that the inhabitants could have free communication with each other.

We hoped to be more successful in obtaining cocoanuts and other vegetable productions at the next island at which we might touch. We made it the following day, but here also we were disappointed. It was a perfect lagoon island, consisting of a circle of land of a light clay colour, the lagoon of a beautiful blue tint. The highest ground was not more than twelve feet above the level of the sea, and we calculated that it was about six hundred feet wide to its lagoon. The shrubs were not numerous, seldom more than twelve to fifteen feet high. Amid them rose conspicuously cocoanut-palms, and pandanus. There was but one narrow entrance into the lagoon; but, from the surf breaking on either side of it, Harry considered that it would be dangerous to attempt passing through. We already knew that, however beautiful a coral island looks at a distance, the landing on it is very disappointing. In order to obtain cocoanuts we pulled for the shore on the lee side, where it seemed possible to land. As we approached the beach, however, we saw a large number of natives collected, and as we drew near they began shouting, gesticulating, and brandishing their long spears and clubs, making violent motions to us to retire. We had a white flag, which we waved, hoping they would understand that it was an emblem of peace, but they took no notice of it, and still threatened to attack us should we attempt to land. We therefore kept off at a respectful distance, and directed Tom Tubb, who could generally make himself understood, to address them. He singled out the chief, and told him that we were friends of the natives, and that we came simply to traffic. The chief merely shouted and gesticulated as fiercely as before, making signs to us to be off, evidently not wishing to have any intercourse with strangers. This enraged the New Zealander, who, standing up in the bow of the canoe, became as much excited as the chief, brandishing the boat-hook as a spear, and making as if he would throw it at him. Thus they continued for some time, till I thought it prudent to desire Tom to cease, but he showed no inclination to do this, evidently taking pleasure in exciting the chief to the greatest pitch of fury. The rest of the natives becoming as enraged as their leader, presently began to assail us with pieces of coral, the only missiles they possessed. To avoid them we pulled away as rapidly as we could: indeed, as it was, several lumps of coral struck the boat. Here again was another proof that the natives had cause to dread an intercourse with white men.

The wind heading us we were compelled to make a tack to the eastward, when we sighted another lagoon island, on which, near the entrance, we saw a flag waving in the air, and near it a number of natives, all more or less dressed in shirts and trousers of various colours. They had no arms in their hands; and as we approached the entrance of the lagoon in a boat they came down to welcome us in a most friendly way. We were not long in discovering the cause, a native neatly dressed in shirt, trousers, and jacket, with a hat on his head, approaching, introduced himself as a native teacher. He could speak a few words of English; and, with the aid of Tom Tubb, we managed to carry on a conversation. He had been only two years on the island. When he first landed the people were as savage as those we had last visited. The whole had now become Christians, and partly civilised. Anxious as he was to instruct them in the truths of Christianity, he was also desirous of improving their social condition. All the women were dressed in cotton gowns, the men as I have described; while their huts were of a superior construction to those on any of the neighbouring islands. The missionary assured us also that many of the people could read, and some could even write. We agreed that should we have the misfortune to be wrecked, how thankful we should be to find that we had been thrown on an island inhabited by these Christian people, instead of such savages as those we had before met with. They supplied us with as many cocoanuts as they could spare. The missionary was instructing them how to make cocoanut oil, that they might be able to purchase with it such articles as they required, I may here remark that there are now very many islands which can rarely be visited by English missionaries, where native teachers have been the means of producing similar results. The next day we fell in with another similar island, in which a native teacher had a short time before landed. He had not been there more than a month or two when a vessel was wrecked which had some time before carried off several of the natives, and, undoubtedly, the only one of her crew who reached the shore would have been put to death had it not been for his interference. He not only saved the man's life, but endeavoured to instruct him in the truths of religion. For this, however, the fellow was far from grateful, for by his conduct he did much to impede the efforts of the teacher. The latter, when we went on shore, entreated us to take the man, who called himself Sam Pest, away with us. Harry, for the sake of the teacher, undertook to do this, if Pest was willing to go. When the question was put to him, he said that he had no objection, provided we would land him at some other island where he might do as he pleased. Harry would make no promise as to where he would land him, notwith-standing which the man came willingly on board; and we bade farewell to the missionary and his flock. Sam Pest had been knocking about the Pacific for the last twenty years he told me, sometimes on board whalers, at others serving in smaller craft, frequently living on shore among the heathen natives. He was, I found, a regular beachcomber—a name generally given to the vagabond white men who are scattered about in numbers among the islands of the Pacific, to the great detriment of the natives, as by the bad example they set them they interfere much with the proceedings of the missionaries. Pest was not so bad, perhaps, as many; he had frank manners, was certainly no hypocrite, for he was not at all ashamed of the life he had led. He had served on board vessels engaged in carrying off natives to work in the mines of Peru, and he gave me many accounts of the atrocious ways in which they had been kidnapped. Sometimes the poor islanders were enticed on board under the pretence of trading, others were carried off by force. On several occasions when canoes had come alongside, the men were dragged out of them, and the canoes sunk. In some instances whole islands had been depopulated, when, from the smallness of their number, the inhabitants were unable to defend themselves against the attacks of the kidnappers.

W. H. G. Kingston

I believe there is some soft part of the human heart, if it can be got at. By the way I talked to Sam Pest, and by occasionally giving him some tobacco, he seemed to take a liking to me. When I pointed out to him the evil of his ways, he acknowledged that he wished he were a better man, and if I would help him, he would try to him over a new leaf. I cannot say that I thought this very likely, from the way I heard him talking to the men.

We had now commenced our search for the Pearl Islands, as Tom Platt asserted we must be close to them. He said that he was certain he should know them again if he could once get sight of them. Now we stood to the northward, now tacked in one direction, now in another, now ran before the wind, carefully marking down our track on the chart, so that we might know what ground we had gone over.

"This reminds me of the long time the missionary Williams was searching for the island of Barotonga before he discovered it," observed Charles Tilston. "He, however, went not to seek wealth for himself, but to carry a pearl of great price to the benighted inhabitants. How I should like to have a vessel and to cruise over the ocean with the same object in view, dropping missionaries here and there as it was found possible to land them."

"Such is being done now," I observed. "I heard a good deal about it at Brisbane, and how the Bishop of New Zealand in his little schooner makes long voyages for that purpose. There are also two or three other vessels employed by different societies with the same object in view."

"I must make inquiries about them," answered Charles Tilston, and he seemed lost in thought.

As we had been four days cruising about without coming in

sight of the wished-for islands, at last Harry began to fear that old Tom had made some unaccountable mistake. He again and again cross-questioned him on the subject. The mate was, however, positive that he was right, and that we should see the islands if we looked long enough for them.

"They may be rather more to the eastward or northward than I fancied, but hereabouts I have no doubt we shall find them," he said in a positive tone.

We accordingly extended our search, keeping always a sharp look-out from the mast-head. Old Tom frequently went up himself, spy-glass in hand, to sweep the horizon. At length, about noon on the sixth day, while he was aloft he raised a cheerful shout—

"Land, land! Away to the eastward; it is the island we are looking for!" As we had a fresh southerly breeze, the schooner was at once headed up in the direction he indicated. In a short time we could make out the land from the deck, which greatly resembled the other islands we had passed, looking like a fleet of vessels at anchor close together. As we stood on we could distinguish several smaller islands lying off the large one, which was the most thickly covered with trees. On getting still nearer we perceived a channel of clear water, along which we hoped to proceed to an anchorage off the larger island of which Tom had told us, and as he had marked it well on his former visit he undertook to pilot the schooner to it. Of course we took the usual precautions of heaving the lead and having a man at the mast-head, and one at each yardarm, while Tom himself stood forward, his hand shading his eyes. The dangers were fewer than we expected, and with infinite satisfaction we at length brought up in a secure harbour.

As we approached it a number of canoes similar to those I

W. H. G. Kingston

have before described, each carrying three men, came off to us. The natives appeared inclined to be friendly, for some were singing a song of welcome, and others waving green branches.

Summoning Tom Tubb and Jacky Pott to act as interpreters, we let the natives understand that we could only admit a dozen on board at a time, and that they must come unarmed. To this they made no objection, but seemed at once perfectly at their ease. From the curiosity they exhibited, they were evidently not accustomed to the sight of vessels in their harbour. They told the New Zealander that they had seen on some time before, which confirmed the account the mate had given of his visit. When told that we came to buy pearls, they appeared in no way surprised, and at once agreed to supply us with as many as we wished for, as also with mother-of-pearl shells; the latter, though bulky, were well worth carrying, as there was at the time much demand for them in the market. My brother at once arranged the price we were to pay, with which the natives seemed perfectly satisfied: they also promised to bring us off a supply of cocoanuts.

As soon as these arrangements were made, they paddled off to spread the good news among their fellow-islanders, and to collect the pearls already won from the bottom of the sea, of which they gave us to understand they had a good store. Before evening the first party returned, bringing a larger number of pearls than we expected. Few of them, however, were particularly fine, but on an average they were of good value, which encouraged us to hope that we should be well paid for our voyage. Notwithstanding the friendly behaviour of the natives, Harry considered it prudent to keep a vigilant watch during the hours of darkness. He told the natives that he should not expect to see them till the next morning.

The night passed away without any cause for alarm. At

daylight the next morning every canoe in the island appeared to be afloat; some brought off pearls, as well as mother-of-pearl shells and cocoanuts, and others were seen paddling out to the water between the reefs where the oyster-beds existed. We carried on a brisk trade for a couple of hours or more. The natives selected the knives and hatchets and other articles they required, and handed over the pearls in exchange. As one party had disposed of their pearls, they were told they must get into their canoes and leave the side of the vessel, while others took their places. Thus there was no confusion, and all went on amicably. The trading over for the morning, as soon as we had breakfasted, Charles Tilston and I, with Dick and two men, pulled off to watch the natives diving for the oyster-shells. About thirty canoes were floating over different spots, each having one diver on board. He had a large net basket fastened round his waist, and, as far as we could see, he was furnished with no other means for obtaining oysters. Standing up in his canoe he drew a deep breath, then, holding his nostrils with one hand, down he dived, and remained below the water for a couple of minutes. On his return his bag was seen to be full of oysters. He had, it appeared, wrenched them off by main force with his hands. The water was so clear that he could see the oysters without difficulty, as he could also the approach of a shark or any other dangerous fish. He remained diving at intervals till his canoe was filled, when she returned to the shore with her freight. I found that the divers select that period of the day for carrying on their operations when the direct rays of the sun illumine the depths of the ocean. On making inquiries through Tom Tubb I found that, notwithstanding the number of sharks which infest those seas, very few of the natives lose their lives from them, as they are always on the watch for the creatures, and know how to elude them with wonderful skill and courage. Every day brought us a fresh supply of pearls, and when we found that it began to fall off we produced some fresh articles to

W. H. G. Kingston

tempt them: gaily-coloured handkerchiefs and cloth, nails, scissors, hammers, gimlets, and similar things. All this time we had not gone on shore. The people were gentle and well behaved on board, but they were heathens and savages, so that it was impossible to tell how they might conduct themselves should they find that we were in their power.

CHAPTER SIX

We had now obtained a fair amount of cargo, and I would have returned to Brisbane well satisfied with our voyage; but Harry, being anxious to get as many pearls as could be procured, resolved to wait on as long as they came in freely and he had goods to pay for them.

Trading was just over for the day, when, looking towards the entrance to the harbour, I saw the topsails of a brigantine appearing over a point to the westward, but as the point was covered with trees, the masts of the schooner could not have been seen from her deck. Her appearance showed us that the island was not so completely unknown as Tom had supposed. I immediately told Harry, who at once proposed sending a boat to assist in piloting her in, and pointing out a good anchorage should she be a stranger. Tom offered to go, and I agreed to accompany him. As we got round the point, we saw that the brigantine was shortening sail, and before we were up to her she had dropped her anchor in mid channel, as if she were not aware of the existence of a harbour, or at all events had no intention of entering it. She was tolerably secure where she lay, and had the advantage of being able to get out again with less difficulty than if she had come into the harbour. We, however, went alongside. She was a rakish-looking craft, and there appeared to be a good many men on board. As we went up her side we saw a swarthy fellow with big whiskers standing to receive us.

"Hulloa, I did not know any other vessel was in here," he said, as we gained the deck. "Where have you come from? What are you about?"

"We hail from Brisbane; we are engaged in trading with the natives," I answered. "And may I ask you in return where you come from, and what is the object of your voyage?"

"We come from Callao, and are engaged as you are," he answered.

I did not like the tone of his voice or manner, and thought it useless asking any further questions. As I looked round the deck it struck me that the people I saw were as ruffianly a crew as I had ever set eyes on, and that the sooner we took our leave the better. I therefore merely observed that on seeing his vessel coming up the channel, supposing that he intended to enter the harbour we had pulled out to offer him our assistance, but that as he did not require it we would wish him good evening.

"I don't like the looks of those chaps," observed Tom, as we pulled away. "They're after no good."

"I do not suppose that they will interfere with us," I remarked.

"I'm not so sure of that," said Tom. "They'll interfere with the natives and spoil our trade; at all events it would be as well to keep a watch on them, and the sooner we are out of their reach the better."

Old Tom was not generally an alarmist; but I did not fancy that even out in the Pacific, in the middle of the nineteenth century, any crew could be found who would venture to commit an act of violence on an English trader when they would be so surely discovered and brought to justice. Still, I fancied that Harry, who was always prudent, would take all necessary precautions. On hearing the account we gave of the trader he, however, to my surprise, laughed at my apprehensions.

"She may not be altogether honest, and I daresay her crew would not scruple to ill-treat the natives; but they will not venture to interfere with us, or to misbehave themselves while we are here to watch them," he observed.

He, however, afterwards, having had a conversation with old Tom, instead of the usual anchor watch at sunset, ordered half the crew to remain on deck, the guns to be loaded, and the small arms placed in readiness for instant use. Sam Pest was in the first watch, and as I walked the deck I spoke to him as I frequently did.

"I have been hearing about the strange craft which came in this evening, sir," he said, "and from what they say I think it's more than likely she's the one I was aboard of some time ago. Strange pranks she played. Her skipper was a regular rough one, never minded what he did, and thought no more of a man's life than that of a dog. I mind what happened once when we were away to the westward after sandal-wood, where the black men of one island are always at war with those of another, and when one side gains the victory never fail to kill and eat their enemies. We had gone to one island where the natives were friendly, and had got them to cut down and bring aboard a good quantity of the wood. When they had cut down all that was to be found in that part of the island, and we had shipped the best part of it, the skipper told them to bring off the remainder in their canoes and he would pay them handsomely. No sooner were they on board than he

W. H. G. Kingston

invited them down into the hold to receive their payment, when he had the hatches clapped on over them, and casting their canoes adrift made sail. He then told them that he was going to take them to another island where there was plenty of sandal-wood, and that when they had cut it down for him and shipped it he would take them back to their own country. This quieted them, though it seemed strange that they should have believed him. In three or four days we got to the island he spoke of, when about half the crew well armed landed with the black fellows, and soon set them to work on the sandal-wood trees, which were some way from the coast. We were on the watch all the time to prevent them or ourselves being attacked by the natives, who kept at a distance, for they dreaded our firearms, as we had shot three or four of them for coming too near. We made our prisoners carry the sandal-wood on their shoulders down to the harbour, when our boats took it on board. We went on in this fashion till we had got a full cargo, notwithstanding which the skipper said he must have the remainder of the wood cut down, and ordered our prisoners to go and fetch it. As they knew the way they trudged on as they had done for several days past. As soon as they were out of sight the skipper told us to give them the slip and return to the boats. On getting aboard he ordered the anchor to be hove up, and sail made, and stood out of the harbour. Just then we saw the sandal-wood cutters come rushing back waving and shouting to us.

"'You must shout louder for me to hear you,' cried the skipper. 'I cannot stop for you.'"

"Presently we saw a whole army of natives with spears and clubs come rushing out of the wood. They soon overtook the runaways, every one of whom was struck down or speared through before they reached the beach.

"That's an easy way of paying our debts," says the skipper,

and that was the only remark he made about the unfortunate wretches who were killed; and as the people in those islands are all cannibals I have no doubt were eaten by the next day.

"This will give you, sir, some notion of the sort of man the skipper was, and if the same man commands the brigantine out there, it's just as well to be on our guard against him."

When I went below to get some supper I told Harry what Sam had said.

"I cannot take more precautions than we are now doing," he answered; "and as soon as we get a breeze to carry us out of the harbour, we'll put as wide a distance as we can between him and ourselves."

It appeared after all, when morning came, that our precautions were unnecessary, not a canoe nor a boat was seen in the harbour; indeed, Harry said that even supposing the crew of the brigantine were the greatest ruffians afloat it was very improbable that they would venture to attack us. Only a few canoes came alongside bringing pearls or oyster-shells. The natives said that if we would wait for a few days they would procure a further supply from some beds at the other end of the island. Harry, however, determined to sail as soon as possible. We now only waited for a fair wind, without which it would have been dangerous to attempt the passage between the reefs.

Breakfast was just over when a boat was seen pulling towards us; she evidently belonged to the brigantine. The guns had been secured, the small arms placed out of sight, and the awning having been rigged, Mary and Fanny were on deck seated with their work in their hands. Presently the boat came alongside, and the skipper whom we had seen the previous evening stepped on deck. Harry received him politely, and begged to know the cause to which he was indebted for a visit from him.

"Just come to learn what you are about, here," answered the skipper in a gruff tone. "I am Captain Samuel Myers. My vessel is the *Wasp*, now belonging to Callao."

"I am happy to see you, Captain Myers; but I thought that my brother, who visited you yesterday evening, had told you that we were on a trading voyage, and about to return immediately to Brisbane."

"What have you been trading in?" asked Captain Myers. "I should not have thought there was much to be got in these islands."

Harry frankly told him, adding, "We have, I believe, obtained all the pearls the natives had collected."

"Where those came from, others may be got," observed the skipper. "I know a trick or two to make the natives work for me; and I should be obliged to you, captain, if you'd show me some of those you have got, that I may see whether they are worth having."

Harry, not liking to refuse, as it would have shown want of confidence in his visitor, told me to bring up one of the cases, as also some specimens of the oyster-shells. I did not think it necessary to select the finest. When Captain Myers saw them his eyes glittered.

"I did not think there were such pearls to be got in these parts," he observed. "Have you many of them, captain?"

"Enough to satisfy me," answered Harry. "Indeed, as I said before, I do not think there are many more to be procured at present."

"We shall see about that," remarked Captain Myers, glancing his eyes round the deck. They fell, I observed, on the guns, and he evidently noted each man of our crew, who had come up to have a talk with the strangers alongside. Harry had not invited any of the latter on board, and I guessed had no intention of doing so.

Captain Myers waited, as if expecting to be asked below to take something, as is usual when one skipper visits another; but Harry, who did not like his appearance more than I had done, apologised by saying that, as the cabin was devoted to the use of the ladies, he could not invite strangers into it; but not wishing altogether to be inhospitable, he ordered the steward to bring up some wine and spirits and biscuits, which were placed in a tray on the companion-hatch. Our visitor, without ceremony, poured out for himself half a tumbler of rum, to which he added a very small quantity of water.

"I like a nip neat at this time of the morning," he observed, as he gulped it down. "It sets a fellow up. Well, as you have got ladies aboard, I won't trouble you with my company any longer," he added, taking another look round the deck. "Good morning to you," and without more ado he stepped back into his boat.

I saw him surveying the schooner as he pulled away. As soon as he was gone, Sam Pest came aft.

"He's the very chap I thought he was, and as neat a villain as ever lived," he said. "I knew him at a glance, but I do not know if he knew me. If he did, he did not show it; but that's just like him, for he is as cunning as need be, and, depend on it, will be up to some trick or other if he thinks he can play it

W. H. G. Kingston

to his own advantage."

I repeated to Harry what Sam Pest had said.

"He must be very cunning to play us a trick while we are on our guard," observed Harry.

We noticed that the brigantine's boat pulled for the shore, her skipper having apparently no fear of the natives. We were now waiting anxiously for a breeze to get out of the harbour, but not a breath of wind stirred its smooth surface. As we were not likely to be able to sail at all events till the evening, when there might be a breeze, some of the men asked leave to go on shore; but Harry, suspecting their object was to have a talk with the boat's crew of the brigantine, refused, and told Tom Platt to find work for them on board.

Captain Myers did not pay us another visit during the day, but we saw his boat pulling back to the brigantine in the afternoon. What he had been about on shore we could not tell, but no more natives came alongside with pearls or oyster-shells, though we saw several canoes paddling out as if about to proceed to the *Wasp*.

"If I was your brother I'd keep a look-out for any trick Captain Myers may be inclined to play," said Sam Pest to me. "He may think that the shortest way of getting a cargo of pearls will be to rob this here schooner, and send her to the bottom."

"You don't mean really to say that you think he is capable of so black a deed," I said.

"I tell you there's nothing he would stick at," answered Sam in a positive tone. "I ain't very particular myself, but I've seen him do things, besides the one I told you of, which made my blood curdle, and heartily wish I was clear of him. I have seen him heave shot into canoes, and sink them alongside the vessel, just to get rid of the natives; and another time when we had some aboard who were somewhat obstreperous when shut up in the hold, he shot them down as if they had been a parcel of rats, and threw some overboard with life still in them. If he does not meddle with us, he'll treat the natives in this place in a way which will make them turn against all white men. For you see they cannot distinguish one from the other; and we shall find it unpleasant, to say the best of it, to remain here."

I heartily thanked Sam for the warning, and assured him that my brother would not forget his good intentions, even though Captain Myers might not act as he thought possible. Of course I repeated what Sam had told me to Harry, when the ladies were not within hearing, for it might have made them unnecessarily anxious. Although my brother was inclined as before to laugh at the idea of Captain Myers attacking us, he took the same precautions as on the previous night. Tom Platt and I had the first watch, with Dick Tilston, Tubbs the New Zealander, and three other men; a couple of hands, besides the officer, would have been sufficient on an ordinary anchor watch. We kept a look-out, by Tom's advice, not only in the direction of the brigantine, but also towards the shore.

"You cannot tell what dodge those chaps may be up to," he observed. "They may come in their own boats, or just as likely aboard a number of canoes, to make us fancy that they are only a party of natives coming off to trade."

Harry and Charles Tilston, with the rest of the men, had gone below, but did not intend to take off their clothes, so that they might be ready to spring on deck at a moment's notice. With all the precautions we had taken I cannot say that I felt

W. H. G. Kingston

particularly anxious; indeed, I must own that I should not have been very sorry if Captain Myers had made an attempt to overpower us. I continued walking the deck, talking to Dick, and occasionally exchanging a word or two with old Tom. The night was calm, and the bright stars shining down from the clear sky were reflected as in a mirror on the surface of the harbour. The only sound heard was the low dash of the sea on the distant reefs, and occasionally some indistinct noise from the shore. My watch was nearly over, and I felt that if my head was on the pillow I should in a moment be fast asleep. Suddenly, as I stopped in my walk, I fancied I heard the splash of oars, but so far off that I could not be certain. I listened, leaning over the bulwarks, with my hand to my ear. Again I heard the sound, more distinctly than before, but though I peered into the darkness I could see nothing. I went across the deck to tell Tom, but he had not heard the sound.

"It may be one of the *Wasp's* boats, but that's no reason why she's coming here," he answered. "However, we'll be on the watch for her, and take precious good care that she does not come alongside for the purpose of doing us harm."

After this I listened, but could hear no sound, and at length fancied that I must have been mistaken. It was just on the point of striking eight bells, and I was leaning over the bulwarks, when I thought I saw two objects through the gloom. I kept my eyes fixed on them. Dick was close to me.

"Look out, and tell me if you see anything," I whispered to him.

"Yes; two boats, and I fancy there's another astern," he answered.

"You're right," I said. "Run and tell the captain, and rouse up the men for'ard; they're not coming at this time of night with any good intentions."

The men were prepared, and every one was on deck in less than a minute, with cutlasses at their sides, pikes in their hands, and the guns cast loose, ready for firing. Three boats now came in sight.

The moment Harry saw them, he shouted at the top of his voice, "Keep off, or we fire and sink you."

Instead of dashing on, as they might have done, the crews of the boats ceased pulling: the threat had had a good effect. They were near enough even now to enable us to send a shot among them; but unless they had given stronger evidence of their intentions of attacking us than they had done, Harry was unwilling to fire. Still it was a critical time; and from the number of men on board the brigantine, we knew that they might possibly overpower us; at the same time, if our men behaved with courage, it was more probable that we should beat them off. Still, it might not be done without bloodshed, if they attacked us with resolution. We had the guns in readiness pointed at them to fire, should they again approach. Harry again shouted—

"We know what you are about; if you come on it will be at your own peril."

No answer was given; still the boats remained on the same spot without advancing.

"Let us give them a shot or two, sir," shouted Tom at the top of his voice. "It will show them we are in earnest."

Scarcely had he spoken when the dark objects receded, becoming less and less distinct, till they disappeared in the darkness. Tom very seldom indulged in a chuckle, but he did so on this occasion.

"I thought as how it would have a good effect," he observed. "They expected to take us by surprise, and had no stomach for fighting. Maybe their skipper wanted them to come on, for he is ready for anything, but the men would not. It's my opinion they are cowards at heart, though boasting knaves when there's no danger."

"What you say, Mr Platt, is very true," I heard Sam Pest remark.

"Well done, Platt," said Harry. "Your words had a good effect. I don't think they'll trouble us again to-night."

"We must not be too sure, sir, of that," said Tom. "Perhaps the skipper will think that towards morning we shall not be keeping so bright a look-out, and may try to steal alongside to surprise us; but he'll find himself mistaken."

As I was very sleepy I went below and lay down, but heard old Tom say that he should remain on deck till daylight. Next morning Harry told me that the boats had appeared, but being hailed to keep off, they had not come nearer, and that he had not thought it necessary to call up all hands as he had done before. Being in the neighbourhood of a pirate, as she was nothing else, was very disagreeable, to say the least of it. Indeed, she in a manner blockaded us, for we could not venture to tow the schooner out to sea lest her boats might attack us in some critical position. Still Harry determined that should we get a leading breeze to sail past her, taking the opportunity of doing so while her boats were away. We saw them passing to the eastward, apparently going to compel the natives to dive for oysters. The calm continued the greater part of that day; but although towards the evening a breeze sprang up, it was too light and not sufficiently favourable to enable us to run out of the harbour. We therefore had to pass another anxious night.

The ladies were not by this time entirely ignorant of what had occurred, but Harry made as light of it as possible; saying that the fellows would not really venture to annoy us, however willing they might be to get possession of our pearls if they could do so without fighting. The third night began; about the middle of the first watch the breeze increased so much, that Harry, who had come on deck, consulted with Tom whether we should get the schooner under weigh, and run past the brigantine in the dark.

"If there was a lighthouse at the end of the reef, and we had a pilot aboard, I would not mind trying it, sir," said Tom. "But you see it would be an awkward job if we were to run ashore; besides, it's just possible that the *Wasp's* boats may be on the look-out for us, and hope to catch us napping this time, though they were wrong before."

Harry said he felt pretty sure of the channel, but the last objection was of more importance, and he determined therefore to wait till daylight. It was settled, accordingly, that as soon as the *Wasp's* boats were seen going in the direction of the oyster-beds, we were to heave up the anchor, and make sail. At the same time, as there might be hands enough left on board the brigantine to attack us, we were to have the guns loaded, and be prepared to defend ourselves if necessary. The remainder of the night passed quietly away; we were thankful to find in the morning a steady and favourable breeze still blowing, which would enable us to run out of the harbour and pass the brigantine without making a tack.

We had just breakfasted, when we saw three boats cross the

mouth of the harbour, and, after pulling in to the shore and waiting for some time, continue their course, accompanied by a number of canoes, to the oyster-beds. As soon as they were out of sight, we hove up the anchor and made sail, as had been arranged. Getting outside, we saw the brigantine lying directly in our course.

"With so many of her crew away, her skipper will not attempt to interfere with us," said Harry.

We were under all plain sail, and, as there was a good breeze, we ran quickly through the water as before, with men on the look-out forward, and the lead kept going. We could almost have thrown a biscuit aboard the brigantine as we passed her. Besides the captain, there were very few men on her deck.

"Good day, Captain Myers," said Harry. "We'll report your whereabouts at Sydney. Have you any message there?"

I need not repeat the answer the skipper gave. It was such as might have been expected from so thorough a ruffian. The next moment, stooping down, he lifted up a musket and presented it at us.

"If you fire so will I," I shouted; but before I could pull my trigger a bullet whistled past my ear. Providentially no one was hit. My bullet also flew wide of its mark; indeed, I was too much hurried to take aim.

"Don't fire again," cried Harry. "The man must be mad."

Probably no other musket was at hand, as the captain of the *Wasp* did not again fire. In a short time we were out of range, and we had too much to do in attending to the navigation of the schooner to think just then much about the matter. From the number of rocks close to which we passed, I was thankful that we had not attempted to run out during the dark. At length we were in the open ocean, and, with a fair breeze, we steered to the westward.

W. H. G. Kingston

CHAPTER SEVEN

The breeze fell before we had entirely lost sight of the Pearl Islands, and, indeed, from aloft I could still make out the masts of the brigantine as she lay at anchor. It crossed my mind that Captain Myers might even now follow us; but I saw no indication of the vessel getting under weigh; still, daring ruffian as he appeared to be, he might be tempted to try and possess himself of the rich freight we carried. I did not mention the idea which had occurred to me to Harry, as there would be no use in doing so, for we were carrying all the sail we could set on the schooner, but our progress was very slow, and there was a possibility of our being becalmed again during the night. As we could see the brigantine, we also must still be visible from her mast-head, and Myers was probably keeping a watch on our movements. Should we be becalmed before sundown, it was possible that he might make another attempt in his boats to capture us, hoping to catch us off our guard.

"He shall not do that, at all events," I thought to myself. "I will not say anything to Harry unless we are becalmed, and then I will tell him the idea which has occurred to me." Our progress was so slow that I fancied there must be a current setting against us, but of this I was uncertain. The currents which set in various directions between the islands of the Pacific are among the dangers which voyagers in those seas have to encounter. I asked Tom what he thought about the matter.

"There may be a current," he said, "but if there is one it is not of much strength. You see we are moving but slowly through the water. We'll heave the log presently, and you'll find that we are not going more than two knots, if as much as that."

Tom was right; with his practised eye he could always tell in smooth water how fast the vessel was moving. We now went slower and slower, till at length the canvas hung down from the yards emptied of wind, and we had no longer steerage way on the vessel. Evening was drawing on, and we might expect to remain becalmed all night. We had, however, we supposed, plenty of sea room, and had no apprehension of being drifted on any unseen coral reef; I thought, however, that it was time to tell Harry of my apprehensions.

"The same thing occurred to me," he answered. "However, I do not really suppose that the fellow Myers, ruffian as he is, will make the attempt after having found us before so wide-awake. Had we been unarmed the case would have been different, as he would have been glad enough to possess himself of our cargo, if he could have done so without the certainty of getting some hard blows. However, we will be on the watch as before, and ready to give his boats a warm reception if they attempt to molest us." We enjoyed our usual pleasant evening meal, and afterwards had music, reading, and lively conversation till bed-time. The mate, meanwhile, kept watch, while I occasionally slipped up on deck to see if there was any prospect of a breeze springing up.

"Not an air in all the heavens," answered old Tom. "It is better than having a westerly gale to drive us back towards the islands. Maybe we shall get a breeze before the morning, and slip along merrily on our course."

W. H. G. Kingston

"I hope so," I said. "The captain wishes you to keep a bright look-out to the eastward, in case our buccaneering friends may be coming to pay us a visit."

"Trust me for that," said Tom. "I have not forgotten them, and the last words the captain spoke to that fellow Myers will make him more than ever eager to prevent our getting to Sydney. I don't mean to say that he will take us, or that he has a chance of taking us, but he is very likely to try it."

After the ladies had retired to their cabins, Harry came on deck.

"I have told them not to be alarmed if they hear us firing, for I am determined should the pirates make their appearance to stand on no terms with them, but, if I can, to send their boats to the bottom before they get up alongside."

"A very right way, too, of treating them, sir," observed Tom. "If we can sink their boats it might be the saving of the lives of many of the poor islanders, for, depend on it, when they have got all the pearl shells they can, they will be carrying off as many of the people as the brigantine can hold. I have seen something of the way those sort of fellows behave, and Sam Pest has been telling me more about it."

The watch on deck were all awake, and the men below had been warned that they must be ready to spring up at a moment's notice; the guns were loaded, and our other weapons were placed handy, ready for use.

As old Tom observed, "If they do not come, there's no harm done; and if they do, why they'll pretty soon find out that they've had their pull for nothing."

As Tom had been awake the whole of the first watch, Harry

told him to go below, observing that he and I would keep a look-out.

"No, thank you, sir," answered Tom; "I will get my sleep by-and-by; I'd like to be ready in case the pirates should follow us."

"You, Ned, had better then go below, as you cannot do without sleep, and you can be called if you are wanted."

I was just about to do as he advised me, when old Tom, pointing to the eastward, towards which our starboard broadside was turned, exclaimed, "As sure as I'm an Englishman there come the boats, and I can make out three of them pulling abreast; we shall see them more clearly presently."

The watch below, which had lately turned in, were soon roused up, and I called Charlie Tilston, as he had begged me to do.

"We will have the port guns over to the starboard side, and give the fellows a salute which will show that we are not to be caught napping," said Harry. "All ready, there?"

He took charge of one gun, Tom of another, Lizard of the third, and I of the last. We waited till the boats had got as far as we could judge within range, and then fired together, aiming as carefully as we could. We then immediately reloaded, to be ready for them should they make a dash at us. Whether or not we had hit either of the boats we could not be certain, they still appeared to be coming on. Just then Harry exclaimed—

"Trim sails; here's the breeze."

The helm was put up, the fore-topsail blew out, the

W. H. G. Kingston

mainsail filled.

"Ease off the main-sheet," cried Harry, and the schooner began to glide once more through the water. We watched the boats now right astern; they still kept following us, hoping not to let their prey escape them. We had two ports in the stern, through which our guns could be fired. Harry had them dragged over for that purpose, and we at once began to blaze away at our pursuers. For some time we could see them still following us, showing that they had hitherto escaped our shot. The breeze was freshening, the schooner ran faster and faster through the water.

"Hurrah! They have given it up," I shouted, as I saw them pulling round.

"One more parting shot," cried old Tom, and before Harry could stop him he fired.

"That was not a miss, at all events," he cried out.

Almost immediately afterwards we could distinguish only two boats—evidence that one of them had been sunk. In a short time we had completely lost sight of them, and all fear of pursuit was over.

We had reason to be thankful that we had avoided a fight, for, desperate as the fellows were, many of us might have been wounded, if not killed, even though we had driven them back; the alternative of their succeeding was too dreadful to contemplate. Harry at once hastened below to assure Mary and Fanny that all danger was over. I now turned in, and though I went to sleep in a moment I kept dreaming all the time that the pirates were boarding us, that we were fighting desperately; sometimes Captain Myers was on deck flourishing a cutlass, singing, "I'm afloat, I'm afloat," and the

"Rover is free," at others, with his cut-throat companions, he was struggling in the water while old Tom was pelting them with marline-spikes.

I was very thankful when I went on deck to find the schooner running on with a fair breeze, and no land anywhere in sight. Mary and Fanny, though they had been naturally very anxious, soon recovered their spirits, and everything went on as pleasantly as could be desired, Charles Tilston was well-informed, and made himself very agreeable, and though he had no intention of becoming a sailor, he soon learned how to take an observation, and could work it out as well as Harry himself. He was always ready also to pull and haul and be as useful as he could. He spent a portion of every day in giving Dick instruction in mathematics and other subjects in which his brother was somewhat deficient, and he also kindly offered to help me with my studies.

As Harry wished to obtain samples of such produce as the islands afforded, he had settled to visit those which were at no great distance from our course to the westward.

The first island we sighted after leaving the Pearl Islands was of considerable size, with a lagoon in the centre. We observed at the south-east end a broad entrance, through which it appeared we might pass without difficulty into the lagoon. Near one side was a village, and the whole island appeared thickly covered with cocoanut and other trees. As from this it seemed probable that we might obtain some palm-oil, the schooner was hove to, and Charlie Tilston and I, with Tom Tubb and three other men, pulled for the shore. As we approached we saw a number of natives rushing down to the beach, all fully armed; but they were not so savage in appearance as those who had prevented us from landing on the islands we had before visited. They shouted and gesticulated, however, making signs that we must not attempt to set foot on shore.

We, however, still pulled on, and as we got closer, Tom Tubb hailed them, and desired to know why they were so inhospitable. They answered—

"We know why you have come. Not long ago a vessel appeared and carried off a number of our people, and you will try to do the same; but we will prevent you."

Our interpreter tried to explain that our object was simply to trade honestly; that if they had any cocoanut oil, we would give them a fair price for it.

"We will not trust you," was the answer. "Go away! Go away!"

As we saw several of the people clothed in shirts, and some even in trousers, we had no doubt that a missionary was among them, though we could not distinguish him from the rest. It was, however, evident that they had been visited by a kidnapping vessel, and some of their people, probably Christians, had been carried off into slavery. Finding, notwithstanding all our protestations that we were honest traders, that the natives would not allow us to land, Charlie and I agreed that it would be folly to attempt doing so, and therefore returned to the vessel.

Soon after this we came off another island totally different to any we had before visited, being formed of corals that had been uplifted to the height of upwards of two hundred feet, and surrounded by cliffs worn into caverns. As no natives appeared, Harry did not wish to lose time by landing.

The islands of the Pacific present a great variety of forms, although the larger number are either partly or entirely surrounded by coral reefs. These reefs, however, vary in construction; some are called encircling reefs, when they appear at a distance from the shore, and a lagoon intervenes; others are called fringing reefs, which are joined to the land, and extend out from it without any lagoon. Others are denominated lagoon islands, when the reef itself, raised above the surface of the ocean, forms the land generally in a circular shape, and surrounds a lake or lagoon, which has sometimes a passage to the sea, and at others is completely closed. Then there are atoll islands; these rise within a large encircling reef, which is seldom perfect, having passages here and there through it. Sometimes there are elevations on the reef itself, forming islands; but frequently the reef is a wash with the sea. Besides these, there are the great barrier reefs which extend along the larger part of the eastern coast of Australia, part of New Guinea, and New Caledonia. Some of these are several hundred miles in extent. These countless reefs are all formed by the coral insect. The difference of their appearance is owing to various causes: some by the subsidence of the land; others by its elevation through volcanic agency. The encircling reefs have been produced by the subsidence of the land; they were originally fringing reefs, having been attached to the coastline of the country or islands. As the land sank, the insects went on building one generation above another; but they can only work in a certain depth of water—below which they die; thus a wall has been built up on the foundations formed by the original workers, who constructed a fringing reef. After a time, the last architects have died, storms have thrown up pieces of coral shells and other debris on the top of the wall, birds have brought seeds of plants, the ocean has washed cocoanuts and other palm seeds on to the top: thus vegetation has been commenced, and finally groves of trees and shrubs have grown up.

The barrier reefs have been formed in the same way. Where

W. H. G. Kingston

no vegetation appears, the has probably sunk as rapidly as the creatures have built, and the sea has continued to wash over it. Other groups have been formed by the violent elevation of the land when the barrier reef has been broken into and wide gaps have appeared.

The last island we visited, surrounded by high cliffs, must have been formed by the sudden upheaval of the earth beneath it, so that the whole mass of coral was lifted above water. Such has been the origin of a considerable number of islands. The most beautiful and picturesque, like Tahiti and others in that group, owe their present shape to the subsidence to the earth, they being merely the summits of mountain ranges, probably of some vast continent, of which the lower land has been submerged. The gaps or openings in the encircling reefs are always found opposite to a river or stream. The coral insect can only build in pure salt water; the fresh water running out from the river has, therefore, prevented its upward progress; thus a gap in the wall has been formed serving as a safe entrance to the inner lagoon. Knowing these facts, it was easy to decide to which class the islands and reefs we passed belonged. There was always, therefore, matter of interest before us.

Volcanic action has been the agent of many of the islands to the westward, where several still active volcanoes exist. Many of those in that direction are clothed with the richest vegetation. They are inhabited by dark-skinned races; still the most savage among those of the Pacific, such as the New Hebrides, Santa Cruz, Solomon Islands, and New Ireland, to the eastward of New Guinea. They produce the finest sandal-wood, and Harry determined to visit some of them, in order to obtain a supply before returning home. He had, however, settled to call first, as I have said, at the islands, where he hoped to be able to purchase palm-oil.

The first we reached after this was very similar to those already described. The natives, as we appeared, came off to the schooner in their canoes, and invited us to enter a secure harbour into which they offered to pilot her. Several of those who boarded us were dressed in shirts, and one of them spoke a sufficient amount of English to make himself understood. He said that two native missionaries were settled on the island, and that all the inhabitants were Christians. They had also, he added, a good quantity of palm-oil, of which they would be glad to dispose. Harry, therefore, without hesitation, accepted their invitation, and we brought up within the outer reef, at no great distance from the shore.

None of the people now cared for the trinkets and other trumpery which they formerly so greatly sought for, but desired to have cotton goods, axes, knives, carpenters tools, fish-hooks, cooking utensils, and other things required by a civilised community. They also asked for paper, pens and ink, and copybooks. We had, unfortunately, no Bibles or other books in their language, or we might have disposed of a good number, so eager were they to procure them. They all behaved, when on board, in a quiet and sedate manner, though they were evidently merry fellows, for we saw them laughing and joking among themselves. Their huts were larger and better built than any we had lately seen, and those we visited were remarkably clean and tidy; yet one of the missionaries whose acquaintance we had made, and who could speak a little English, told us that the people a few years ago were as savage as any of those in that part of the Pacific. We bought a dozen casks of palm-oil at a fair price, calculating the value of the goods we gave in return. The people said if we would come back they would have a further quantity with which to supply us.

We warned them about the *Wasp*, and gave them a minute description of her, so that should she appear they might avoid being entrapped. They replied that they had heard of such vessels cruising about to carry off the natives, but that none had visited their island, and that they had therefore doubted of their existence. They thanked us much for warning them, and promised to be on their guard. We advised them to be cautious how they went on board any vessels before being acquainted with their character.

The next island off which we called was also inhabited by Christian natives, who supplied us with six casks of oil.

I have not space more minutely to describe the islands we touched at. Wherever missionaries were established, there the people were more or less civilised, industrious, and happy. They had not ventured to lay aside their weapons altogether, as they might be required to defend themselves against the nefarious proceedings of lawless white men; but as soon as they found that we came to trade honestly with them, they put them by, and mixed among us without the slightest sign of fear, not even attempting to keep their women out of our sight.

When Mary and Fanny landed, the latter gathered round them, expressing their wonder at their dresses and fair complexions, we felt indeed that we were among friends who could be thoroughly trusted.

Having obtained as much palm-oil as we required, we now steered to the south-west for Vavau, one of the Friendly Islands, of which the civilised King George is the ruler. We made it early in the morning, and, the wind being fair and the harbour easy of access, without waiting for a pilot we stood on, having two small islands on the eastern side, and a larger one to the westward. Vavau appeared of uniform height. At first we did not see many signs of fertility or cultivation; the cliffs rose abruptly from the sea without a fringing reef; but the water had worn the coral rocks, which stand out from the shore, into the shape of huge mushrooms on their stalks. When once we were inside, however, signs of the most industrious cultivation showed themselves. The country was covered with woods, looking like one vast garden, while from every village came the sound of the mallet, used by the women in beating out the native cloth. At a wharf not far off were several large double canoes taking in cargoes for another port; beyond could be seen a number of comfortable-looking houses. Numerous huts of smaller dimensions peeped out from among the trees, while at some distance apart were buildings of considerable size, which we afterwards found to be churches. Altogether we felt that we had come to a civilised country.

Soon after we had dropped anchor, an old native gentleman came off in a large canoe, and introduced himself as the Viceroy of Vavau, and begged to know the object of our visit. Harry replied that he had come to refit the schooner, but should be happy to trade if we could procure any of the articles we required. The old chief said that the people would be ready to receive money as payment for any of their produce, that they had cotton, and palm-oil, and Beche-de-Mer, cocoanuts, native cloth, and various other articles, and that they could supply us with an abundance of hogs and goats, and vegetables of all sorts at a cheap rate.

We were received, as we had been at Samoa, by the white inhabitants in a very kind way, but as Harry was anxious to refit the schooner as soon as possible, the two ladies, under the escort of Charlie Tilston, could alone be much on shore. We, however, managed to see something of the country—the roads in course of construction in all directions across it, the cotton plantations and well-cultivated gardens, and many other signs of the industry of the people. The greatest novelty was the manufacture of the native cloth, or Tapa, formed out of the bark of the paper-mulberry tree. The natives universally wear it for clothing, and as it cannot stand any amount of wet and is easily spoiled, there is a constant demand for it. It is manufactured entirely by the women. The young tree is first cut down and the bark is stripped off; it is then steeped in water for a couple of days, when the inner is separated from the coarse outer rind. This is then beaten by a mallet, resembling a square razor strop with small furrows on the under side, till it becomes almost as thin as silver paper, and of course is greatly increased in size. Even then it is scarcely a foot wide, but the edges are overlapped and stuck together with arrowroot melted in water; it is then again beaten till all the parts are completely joined. Pieces are thus made of many yards in length. A mucilaginous dye is then used, both to colour the cloth, and further to strengthen it, until large bales are formed of a single piece, from which portions are cut off as required for use. Some of those we saw were fifty yards long and four yards wide. When thus formed, it is called Tapa or Taba, a name by which it is generally known among all the islands of the Pacific. It is afterwards beautifully coloured, sometimes by a stamp, at others by painting it by hand, when it is known as Gnatu. A coarser kind, worn by the common people, is made from the bark of the bread-fruit tree.

A number of canoes came alongside, bringing turkeys, fowls, eggs, and a variety of fruits and vegetables, among which were pine-apples, bananas, yams, sweet potatoes, cabbages, and onions. Besides cotton, the natives produce tobacco for their own use, and probably, before long, cotton manufactures will supersede the Tapa. Although the former will be more useful, it has not the elegance of the native cloth.

We visited a chapel built in the native style; it was upwards of a hundred feet long by forty-five wide, and nearly thirty high. It had a high-pitched roof, with curved ends, and two rows of columns, each three of the lower column supported a short beam, from which sprang a second series bearing the ridge-pole. These, as well as the horizontal beam, were beautifully ornamented with cocoanut plait, so arranged as to give the appearance of Grecian mouldings, of infinite variety and delicate gradations of colour—black, with the different shades of red and yellow, being those employed. Altogether the effect was very artistic and pleasing.

The Tongans are said to be the best canoe builders and navigators in the Pacific. One of the chiefs exhibited, with some pride, a large double canoe, which consisted in the first place of a canoe a hundred feet in length, and half a dozen or more in width; the second canoe was composed of a tree hollowed out for the sake of buoyancy like the canoe, but was, in reality, merely an outrigger. The large canoe was formed of planks lashed together with cocoanut plait; beams were then laid between the two, on which was erected a house for the stowage of provisions; above this rose a platform surrounded by a railing, forming the deck of the vessel. It had been built by Tongans in the Fijis, where suitable timber could alone be procured. These vessels, frail and unwieldy as they appear, are navigated in the face of the trade wind between two and three hundred miles, the Tongans making voyages to Fiji and also to Samoa. We were told that six years are required to build one. The sail, formed of matting, is triangular, spread on a long yard. The vessel is never tacked, but the sail is lowered, shifted over, and again hoisted when beating to windward.

We made the acquaintance of a young chief—greatly resembling our Samoan friend Toa—who offered to show us some interesting caverns which exist along the coast. The distance was too great for the ladies to venture, as we had to perform the voyage in a small canoe, and should be away the whole day; but Harry told Charlie and Dick Tilston, Nat and me, that we might go.

We started at daylight in two canoes, with an ample supply of provisions on board, Nat and I accompanying the young chief Alea. He could speak a little English, and gave us an interesting legend connected with one of the caves.

Years ago, a chief had rebelled against the king of the country, when, being defeated, he and his family were condemned to death. He had a very beautiful daughter, who had a lover belonging to another family. Having gained intelligence of the intention of the king to exterminate the family of his beloved, he hastened to her, and managed, without being discovered, to carry her on board a small canoe which he had in waiting. She asked how he could possibly hope to escape by such means from the vengeance of the king, who would destroy him as well as herself. He told her not to fear—that he had a place of concealment, where, notwithstanding the most vigilant search which could be made for her, she would never be discovered. They paddled away till they reached a cliff which rose out of the water.

"I see no cavern in which I can be concealed," she said.

"Fear not; I will conduct you to one, notwithstanding," he answered, and, taking her hand, desired her to leap overboard.

Trusting him to the full, she obeyed; and, both diving, they swam for some distance, till they rose in the centre of a large cavern with rocks, free of water, on one side of which there was sufficient space to rest. Here he told her that she might remain secure, and that he would bring her food every night, till he could make arrangements for their escape to Fiji. He had discovered the cavern, he said, not long before, when diving for a turtle. He was unable to fulfil his promise till he came, one night, and told her that a large double canoe, with friends of his, was waiting outside. They were soon on board, and arrived safely in Fiji, where they remained till the death of the king enabled them to return to Vavau. From this legend Byron draws a romantic account of Neuha's Cave in his poem of "The Island."

As our friend had not described the first cave to which he took us, we were surprised and delighted with it. The mouth was of considerable width, sufficient to admit two or three boats abreast. Once inside, the water was fully five fathoms deep. We here found ourselves amid columns and stalactites hanging from the high-domed roof, resembling Gothic arches. The bright sunlight streamed down through the wonderfully clear water, and was reflected up from the sparkling stones and coral at the bottom, with a beautiful series of light tints, and shades of delicate blue and green, over every part of the walls and vaulted roof. We agreed that it was the fit abode of the most charming of sea-nymphs and mermaids; indeed, we almost expected to see some of the fair ladies seated among the rocks, combing their hair. At the further end there was an arched passage, sloping upwards till it reached an opening in the roof above. Some of our companions landed, and made their way up it, now appearing, now disappearing among the rocks, the effect in their progress being singularly picturesque and scenic. On their return, after visiting another smaller cave, we made sail for Neuha's cavern. On arriving at the spot, we in vain looked for any sign of the entrance, till the chief pointed out to us two poles placed crosswise, which, he said, marked it.

"Now, which of you would like to accompany me into the cavern?" he asked. "You must be prepared for a long dive."

Neither Charlie nor Dick Tilston were willing to venture, on hearing how long they would have to hold their breath. At last I agreed to go, the chief undertaking to keep hold of my hand, and to conduct me in safety. On looking down, with our backs to the sun, we could see a darker patch than usual among the coral-covered rocks, some eight feet below the surface: this was the entrance. We had brought a long line, which was secured to one of the canoes. A follower of the chief's, taking the end, jumped overboard. By watching him carefully we saw him disappear in the midst of the dark patch. He was absent for about ten minutes, and he said that he had made the line secure in the inside of the cavern. After he had rested a little while, the chief asked me if I was ready, when, he and his follower taking me by the arm, we dived downwards, the chief keeping the end of the line in his hand to guide us. I held my breath and struck out with my feet, but my companions had some difficulty in keeping me down sufficiently to avoid scraping my back against the sharp points which project from the roof of the passage. As the whole distance was thirty feet, I was so much exhausted by the time I reached the surface inside the cavern that I could not at first admire its wonders. My companions helped me to a ledge of a rock just visible in the dusk, where we stopped to rest ourselves. The subdued light within the cave was derived entirely from the reflection through the mouth of the submerged passage, and I was at first afraid that I should scarcely be repaid the exertion I had made and the risk run. Suddenly, however, the chief leaped into the water, and began swimming about, when the phosphorescent light produced by his movements was more beautiful and brilliant than anything of the sort I had ever seen. Wherever he went he was followed by a stream of liquid fire. When both the natives were in the water, the light was sensibly increased, so that I obtained some notion of the size of the cavern. It was, however, at the best, a somewhat dreary place of captivity, and the poor girl who inhabited it must have passed many an anxious hour, uncertain whether her lover would be able to return and bring her her daily allowance of food and water, and help her finally to escape. I owned that, having once performed the feat, I did not feel that I should be inclined to pay the cave a second visit. I therefore, as I sat on the rock and pictured to myself how the lovely Neuha had passed her time, took in every visible object; then, feeling rested, told the chief that I was ready to return to the outer world. I own that I had some slight apprehension of encountering a shark on the way; but I felt tolerably satisfied that my companions would send it to the rightabout, if they did not kill the monster.

"Now I'm ready," I said.

The natives then, seizing my arms as before, dived with me almost to the bottom, and, while holding my breath, I felt myself carried along, this time escaping the roof. With infinite satisfaction I saw the bright sunlight overhead. We rose to the surface close to the canoe, and I was hauled on board, pretty well done, however, to receive the congratulations of my friends. The account I gave did not tempt them to make the experiment. After landing on some rocks to discuss the viands we had brought, we pulled back the way we had come, and late in the evening got on board the schooner.

W. H. G. Kingston

CHAPTER EIGHT

We were now bound on a cruise among the islands of Melanesia, inhabited by a dark-skinned race, differing very greatly from the people we had previously visited. We hoped, however, to obtain a supply of sandal-wood, and to establish friendly relations at different spots, so that the schooner might return for another cargo, and bring back any natives who might be willing to engage as labourers in Queensland. Had time allowed, we should have been glad to touch at Fiji, the inhabitants of which were by that time no longer to be dreaded—many, with their old king, Thakombau, once a cannibal, having been converted to Christianity, and partially civilised—but Harry was anxious to conclude the voyage, which had already been longer than he had at first intended.

We had been some days at sea when we came in sight of Cherry Island, rising some three hundred feet above the surface of the ocean, and thickly covered with vegetation, but only two miles and a half in circumference. It appeared truly a little gem in the midst of the world of waters. As there were no dangers off it, we were able to stand close enough in to observe the fine sandy beach extending round it for a considerable distance. Along the shore we saw no canoes, but a number of natives appeared, waving green branches— emblems of peace. As we watched them through our telescopes, we saw that they were of the Polynesian, or brown race—fine-looking fellows, unlike the Papuans, who inhabit the islands we were about to visit. As it was not likely that they could supply us with either cocoanut oil or sandal-wood, we did not communicate with them, but continued our course westward.

The first island we made after leaving Cherry Island, was Varikoro, one of the Santa Cruz group, but, as we were bound northward, we did not heave to till we came off the small island of Lom-lom, where we saw a number of canoes paddling towards us. The natives who manned them wore rings in their ears and noses. Though their object was to trade, as they brought off only a few bows and arrows, and a fruit in appearance and taste resembling an apple, we soon concluded our transactions with them.

Thence standing on, and passing several other islands, the next day but one we reached that of Nukapu, which has a melancholy interest, as it was here that the excellent Bishop Patteson lost his life. The island itself appeared to be about a couple of miles in circumference, and is surrounded by a coral reef, extending, on its south-west side, as far as a mile and a half from the shore, but in other places much nearer. The island was covered with a dense bush, growing down to within a few feet of the water's edge. As we were not aware at the time of the treacherous character of the natives, while the schooner was hove to, Charlie and I, with four men as a crew, pulled off in the gig, hoping to open up an intercourse with them. We were well armed with muskets, pistols, and boarding-pikes, in case we should be attacked. On approaching the reef, we saw a number of canoes floating in the lagoon, each containing three men. We found, however, that we could not get over the reef, but we saw the people on the beach waving green branches, inviting us to come on shore. We accordingly pulled in, believing that we should meet with a friendly reception. As, however, we got near, the savages commenced yelling and dancing in a curious fashion.

"They wish to do us honour, I suppose," said Charlie. "It will be wise, however, not to trust them too much."

We pulled on till we got to within a hundred yards of the beach.

"Look out; they mean mischief!" I shouted; and scarcely were the words out of my mouth when a flight of arrows came whistling towards us, though, fortunately, they fell short of our boat. In vain we tried to make the natives understand that our object was peaceable, by waving white handkerchiefs, and holding up our hands without exhibiting our weapons. This only made them yell and dance more furiously than before. We might have shot down a number of the natives, but we did not for a moment think of doing that, and therefore at once returned to the schooner.

We now continued our course until, towards evening, we came in sight of a lofty mountain, rising in a conical form out of the ocean. On turning our glasses towards its summit, we could see dense volumes of smoke and flame issuing forth, and as it lay in our course, and the wind was fair, we passed close to it. When darkness came on, the whole summit of the mountain appeared to be a mass of fire. Harry summoned Mary and Fanny, who had gone below, on deck to enjoy the magnificent spectacle. Now flames would shoot forth, rising high in the air; and then the incandescent lava, flowing over the edge of the crater, would come rushing down the slope of the mountain, finally to disappear in the sea. Then again all was tolerably quiet. Now we heard a loud rumbling noise, and presently the lava bubbled up once more, to plunge as before down the mountain-side.

"I'm very glad we are no nearer," observed Nat. "Suppose we were to be driven by a gale of wind against it, we should run the double chance of being burnt up by the lava or drowned among the breakers."

"We'll take good care to keep away from it, then," said Harry, laughing.

The following day we came off the island of Santa Cruz, the largest of the group. When even several miles from the shore, a number of canoes approached us, each generally containing three people, all of whom showed an anxiety to trade. We stood into a small harbour, where we brought up, when immediately more than a hundred canoes came around us, loaded with mats, bows and arrows, and cocoanuts, which the islanders willingly gave for bottles, pipes and tobacco, and for articles of clothing. Whenever a shirt or a pair of trousers were to be had, the islanders immediately slipped them on, not always as they were intended to be worn, several putting the hind part before. They were an ugly race—their skins nearly black, and their foreheads low and receding, with high cheekbones and broad faces, their noses flat and mouths large, while their heads were like black, curly mops. I cannot exactly say that they were dressed, their only garment being a sort of apron, fastened by a string tightly round the waist; but they wore tortoise-shell rings hanging from their ears down to their shoulders, and one large ring through the nose, which gave a most hideous expression to their countenances. Some had on necklaces of human teeth, and armlets of shells. Their habitations were low, small, and dirty huts of a circular form, roofed with the leaf of the cocoanut tree, and destitute of every description of furniture. They were altogether the most ugly and diminutive race we had hitherto met with.

As usual, Harry would only allow a dozen on board at a

W. H. G. Kingston

time, while a strict watch was kept on all their movements, but as far as we could judge, they had no treacherous intentions. As evening approached, we made them understand that we wished to be left in quiet, though it was somewhat difficult, without giving them offence, to get them into their canoes. They then paddled on shore, promising the next day to return with the sort of wood we required, of which we showed them a specimen. We, of course, kept a strict watch during the night, and were ready at any moment to defend ourselves; but not a single canoe was seen floating on the surface of the harbour; we therefore supposed that the natives had retired to their huts to sleep.

Next day a chief came off, the distinguishing mark of his rank being a breastplate of white shells, about nine inches in diameter. He brought with him several large bundles of sandal-wood, and promised, if we would come again some time afterwards, to procure for us as much as we required. Savage as these people were, they seemed willing enough to trade, and there is no reason to doubt that the blessings of Christianity might be introduced among them. Such is the task undertaken by the Melanesian Mission, about which Charlie Tilston often talked to me.

We soon after this came off Sugar-Loaf, or Mota Island, which is the head-quarters of the Melanesian Mission; and, as Harry thought the missionaries would be glad of an opportunity of sending letters by us, he ordered a boat to be got ready to go on shore, while the schooner was hove to. I went in her, with Charlie and Dick, Jack Lizard, Tom Tubb, Jackie Potts, and Sam Pest. On approaching the beach, we found it was rocky and rugged, while so heavy a surf was seething on it, that we were afraid to attempt landing; we therefore pulled round, hoping to reach a part where we might get on shore without danger. Rounding a point, we lost sight of the schooner, and after going some distance, succeeded in finding a sheltered nook, into which we ran the boat.

Leaving Dick in charge of her, Charlie and I proceeded on foot in search of the missionaries' houses. The walk was a much longer one than we had expected, but we at last found them, and were courteously received. They expressed themselves very grateful for the attention Harry had shown them, and immediately set to work to write letters, while their wives prepared some refreshments for us. They also insisted upon sending some down to the boat. We in the mean time walked out to a spot whence we expected to see the schooner, but when we got there, great was our dismay at not being able to discover her. A dark cloud, sending down a deluge of rain, was sweeping over the ocean, driven evidently by a heavy squall.

"We shall see her when it has passed over," observed Charlie; "for she will then stand back should she have been driven away from the land."

"I trust so," I said. "Harry is always cautious, and would have shortened sail in time; otherwise the squall has strength enough to capsize her or whip the masts overboard."

"You should not allow such a fancy to enter your head," he observed, wishing to comfort me, as I felt fearfully anxious.

We kept watching the spot where the schooner ought to have been, entirely forgetting the repast prepared for us. The cloud seemed to increase in size, the rain grew thicker and thicker.

"If the schooner is still afloat, she must be in the very midst of it," I at length observed, with a groan.

"Of course she is," said Charlie, "and running before it. She could not possibly beat back in the teeth of such a squall. We shall see her when it has passed."

When we looked back landward, we saw, however, that the sun was already sinking below the tree-crowned heights, and in that latitude darkness comes on almost immediately after the sun has gone down. Still, we could not tear ourselves from the spot.

We were standing thus when we heard a voice saying, "I have been searching for you, my friends, for a long time, and could not conceive where you had gone."

Charlie explained the cause of our anxiety, for I was too much agitated to speak.

"Trust in God's mercy, my friends," said the missionary. "We must hope that your vessel has not suffered material damage, though you do not see her. If she has been dismasted, which is possible, you would scarcely discern her at the distance she must be off by this time. Her captain must undoubtedly have perceived the squall coming, and would be prepared to encounter it."

All he could say, however, did not relieve my anxiety. He waited with us till the gloom of evening, stealing over the eastern ocean, made us abandon all hope of discerning the vessel. We then returned with him to his house, where we were thankful to take the refreshment his wife had prepared. We hurried it over, as we wished to get back as soon as possible to the boat.

"I have sent to say that you are delayed," remarked the missionary, "and I must urge you not to attempt to put to sea till the morning. You would very probably miss your vessel in the dark, whereas she is sure to stand back to look for you at daylight. I must advise you to wait till then. Have your boat hauled on shore, and let your people come up here to pass the night, as this elevated position is more healthy than on the lower ground; and I will take care that an efficient guard is placed to protect her."

This advice was so good that we were fain to accept it. We therefore returned with the missionary to his house, while he despatched a New Zealander, who spoke English, to bring up Dick and the men. Having a guide, they were much less time reaching the station than we had been, and soon arrived. Of course, Dick was very much grieved to hear of our anxiety about the schooner. The missionaries and their wives did their best to draw our thoughts away from our friends, by describing the progress of the work they had undertaken. Their object was, they told us, to collect young and intelligent natives from the different islands, and to endeavour to instruct them in the truths of Christianity. When their education was completed, if they exhibited a right missionary spirit, they were sent back to diffuse the truths of Christianity among their fellow-islanders.

It was deeply interesting to see a number of natives brought from among the most savage races, gentle and civilised, and apparently imbued with true Christian principles. They were all clothed in shirts and trousers, and looked as different as possible to the savages we had met with, though of the same race, and a few years ago were exactly like them.

We sat up for some time, hoping against hope that we might hear a gun fired from the schooner, as a signal to us that she was in the offing. Several times we looked out over the ocean, now sleeping in calm repose, but no sign of the schooner could be discovered.

At last the missionary advised us to take some rest. He had a

W. H. G. Kingston

guest-room in which, he said, beds were prepared for Charlie, Dick, and me, while some shake-downs of leaves and grass were made up in an outhouse for the crew of our boat. I kept continually starting up, fancying that I heard a gun fire. Again when I slept I pictured to myself vividly the schooner struck by the squall, and going down beneath the surface.

As soon as morning broke we were all on foot, and hurried to the look-out place, whence we earnestly hoped that we might see the schooner; but not a sail was in sight above the distant horizon. The Christian converts were gathered for prayer, and we joined them, though unable to understand what was said. When our early breakfast was over, I again hurried out to look for the schooner. Still, as far as eye could reach, there was no appearance of her. I felt that, as I was in command of the boat, I must decide what was to be done, though I wished to consult my companions and have their opinion. I proposed that we should, without loss of time, proceed in the boat to some of the neighbouring islands to search for her, believing it possible that she had been compelled to take shelter in one of their harbours. I told Charlie what I thought of doing.

"Dick and I will be ready to accompany you, whatever you may decide," he answered.

"Then let us go at once," I said. "We have a sail in the boat, and, though the distance between the islands is considerable, we may cross in a few hours from one to the other."

When we told the missionary what we intended to do, he strongly urged us to remain with him for a day or two, in the hope that the schooner might in the mean time return.

"The vessel may be on one side of the island, and you may be passing on the other and thus miss her," he observed.

I thanked him very much, but still told him that I was too anxious to commence our search to delay a moment longer than necessary. As the schooner carried another gig, my brother was certain to send on shore, should we miss each other, to inquire for us, and we agreed to return should we fail to find him.

"If you insist on going, I must beg you to allow me to supply you with provisions and water," said our kind friend, "and I must advise you to be very cautious in attempting to land on any of the islands. You must remember that they are inhabited by treacherous races, on whom no dependence can be placed. It will be better to endure hunger and thirst than to run the risk of being clubbed, should you land among hostile natives."

I again thanked him heartily for his kindness, and assured him that we would be as cautious as necessary. Bidding him and his companion and their wives farewell, we went down to the boat, accompanied by a number of natives carrying the provisions with which we had been furnished. Our boat was launched, and we put to sea.

CHAPTER NINE

We had what might prove a long and dangerous voyage before us, while we were almost overwhelmed with the anxiety we felt about the fate of the schooner. We could see the first island we intended to visit just rising out of the water, blue and indistinct, and as it was calm we had to depend upon our oars to reach it, but we hoped before long to get a favourable breeze which would send us on our way. The sun struck down on our heads with intense force, but we were too anxious to think about it. I proposed that we should relieve each other at the oars, so that we might continue pulling, if necessary, all day. Jack Lizard, Potts, and Tubb declared that they would not allow us to do that.

"If you like to change places now and again with Dick, and his brother takes a turn with the oar, it is all very well; but we are born to it, as it were, and it makes no difference to us if we pull on all day," said Jack.

Fortunately, after we had pulled a couple of hours and the island of Mota was fading in the distance, a breeze sprang up, and we were able to stand on under sail. At length, towards evening, we got near the shore, and seeing a number of natives on the beach, we hoped that we might obtain information from them as to what had become of the schooner; for, had she been driven past the island, they must have seen her.

"We take care," said Tubb, the New Zealander. "I not like dere looks; dey not friends."

The people had hitherto been quiet enough, and I had observed no signs of hostility; no sooner, however, did we approach the shore than they assumed a warlike attitude, dancing and gesticulating in the wildest manner, while they yelled and brandished their weapons as a sign to us that we were to come no nearer. As it would have been madness to have attempted landing in the face of such hostile demonstrations, we put the boat partly round, and pulled on parallel with the shore, but at a respectful distance. As we did so, we saw the natives running along the beach, every now and then making threatening gestures as a warning to us not to land.

"They may be savages," observed Charlie; "but they cannot be called treacherous ones, or they would have allowed us to land and afterwards murdered us."

We continued along the coast, hoping to come to the mouth of some harbour in which we might find the missing schooner. No harbour appeared, and everywhere, whenever we stood in closer than before to the beach, the natives, gathering in numbers, ordered us to keep off. We had now no choice but to remain at sea during the night, for we could not hope to reach the next island within several hours. We therefore stood away from Inhospitable Island, as we called it.

Fortunately the weather remained fine, and the coolness of the night was pleasanter than the heat of day. A distant volcano, which threw up a continuous column of flame, enabled us to steer a direct course, and, as the breeze was very light, we did not expect to reach Aurora Island, which we intended next to visit, till morning. Jack Lizard and I took it by turns to steer, for I was rather afraid of trusting Charlie Dick Tilston, lest a sudden squall might strike the boat and send us over. Our minds were too much occupied with the thoughts of the schooner, or rather of those on board her, to enable us to talk on any other subject Charlie Tilston every now and then tried to get up a lively conversation, but found that he could not succeed. All night long we glided smoothly on.

"I hope that we shall be treated in a more hospitable way by the inhabitants of the next island we visit," he observed.

"We cannot be very certain about that, sir," observed Sam Pest. "I have been up and down these islands, and I have seen the way white men have treated the blacks. No wonder they ain't friendly, for there's not a village scarcely where some of the natives have not been carried off, while others have been fired on and the people killed. We must make them understand that we come as friends, or we shall have no chance of getting anything out of them."

By daylight we were close up to Aurora Island. The inhabitants had seen our boat approaching, and had gathered on the beach to receive us. They probably thought that our vessel was not far off, round a point to the westward.

"Come, I think we have a chance of a friendly intercourse with these people," observed Charlie; "and if you like, I will land and try to have a talk with them by signs. Neither Tubb nor Potts seem to understand their language better than we do."

Although the natives waved no green boughs, and kept a short distance back on some high ground above the beach, yet, as their women and children were with them, and as they made no hostile demonstrations, we concluded that we might safely land. We therefore ran the boat on to the beach, and Charlie, stepping out, moved a few paces from them, and sat down on a rock. In a short time six or seven persons came down to where he was sitting, apparently inclined to hold a palaver, Sam Pest all the time watching them narrowly.

"Take care, sir," he shouted, "or they'll play you some foul trick." The next instant he added, "Jump up! Run for your life down to the boat!"

As he spoke I seized a musket, and old Sam took up another and presented it at the natives, to cover Charlie and enable him to get back to the boat. Just as he sprang up, I saw a young native in the act of lifting a club as if about to strike him; but the suddenness with which Charlie started up and retreated to the boat prevented the savage from dealing the intended blow. Charlie springing on board, we shoved off, and lay on our oars at a safe distance from the beach. This was a bad commencement, and there seemed but little chance of our obtaining any information from them. When the natives saw our guns pointed at them, they quickly retreated, and though we did not fire, and made signs to them to return, nothing would induce them to trust themselves near us.

"I am afraid, from what Sam says, that we can expect no better reception wherever we go. But we must not complain of the poor natives," observed Charlie; "they are thorough savages, it is true, but would probably have received white men with gladness, if the white men had from the first treated them properly, and tried to win their regard."

"That may be so," I remarked. "But we must not forget how the far less savage inhabitants of the Friendly Islands treated the shipmates of Mariner, and would, it is said, have treated

Captain Cook and his companions, if they had had the opportunity. Their conduct, in some instances, is owing to debased human nature, rather than to a spirit of revenge, though undoubtedly in many the white men have been the aggressors."

Finding that we were not likely to establish a friendly intercourse with the natives, or to gain any information about the schooner, we pulled away from the beach, and steered before the wind for another island which we saw to the westward. Although our hearts were full of anxiety, and our thoughts were occupied with the task in which we were engaged, we could not help admiring the beauty of the islands amid which we were sailing. We found the water very deep round the beach, from which the hills rose abruptly, clothed with a dense vegetation. Cocoanut trees grew in the greatest profusion, not only on the shores, but frequently up the sides of the hills, and were seen in clusters at the bottom of the valleys running inland. There were also many other fine timber trees, while graceful ferns and flowering shrubs formed a dense undergrowth over all the uncultivated parts of the country. The water was so transparent that we could see the fish swimming about as we looked over the side of the boat. We had, fortunately, some hooks and lines, and as nearly anything served for bait, we were able to catch as many as we could possibly eat. The difficulty was to cook them, as we could not venture to land on any spot where there were natives. Our fear also was that we might run short of water; thus, although in the midst of abundance, we might perish of thirst, or by the hands of the savages.

"We must manage to land somewhere," cried Dick. "Perhaps if we were to pull in to the shore towards evening, we might escape detection, and have time to cook our fish and find water before the natives are down upon us."

"Although there may be some risk, I do not see what else we can do," said Charlie. "We must, however, keep a strict watch while we are cooking our food, and not attempt to sleep on shore. We shall probably be able to obtain some cocoanuts in addition to the water, so that we may keep at sea, without the necessity of landing again, for several days."

As this plan seemed feasible, we determined to adopt it.

"The island out there, for which we are steering, is of considerable size, and there must surely be some parts uninhabited," observed Charlie.

"I hope so," I said. "As there are a good many missionaries scattered about, we may drop upon some island where one is established; and, if so, we shall be better off than we should if we landed at an uninhabited part; besides which, we may possibly gain tidings of the schooner."

The breeze was light, but yet sufficient to enable us to run on under sail. We had miscalculated the distance to the island, for, the hills being high, it appeared nearer than it really was. We were still some way off the shore when the sun set; the wind also fell, and we had to lower the sail and take to our oars. This, however, was the best thing we could do, as we had less chance of being seen, should there be any people on the shore. The moon rose as we neared the land, and gave us sufficient light to distinguish objects, so that we might pick out a place into which we could run the boat. Seeing no fires or lights, we began to hope that we should not meet with natives; we therefore pulled in, placing Tubb ahead to look out for rocks. The part we first made appeared too rugged to allow us to venture on; we therefore rowed along the shore for some way, till a small sandy bay, just suited to our purpose, appeared. We accordingly steered in for it, keeping, as before, a careful look-out ahead. The ground rose abruptly almost immediately beyond the beach, on which no surf was breaking; but I fancied that I heard a rushing sound of water falling probably over the cliffs close at hand, though a thick grove of tall trees concealed it from our sight.

"We could not have discovered a better place," said Charlie, in a cheerful tone. "We may here remain securely till morning, and get some sleep without being cramped up in the boat. I should not be surprised either if those are cocoanut trees, and, if so, we may get a good supply."

We now rowed into the bay, Tom Tubb feeling the way with the boat-hook, so that we might not run the risk of staving in the bows of the boat. At length our keel grated on the smooth sand, and jumping out, we quickly hauled up the boat. Tubb and Sam Pest then went on, the latter carrying a musket, to survey the neighbourhood, and to ascertain if there was any path by which an enemy might come suddenly down and surprise us; they were also to look out for water. We meantime collected driftwood and dry branches from under the trees to make a fire. We placed a pile some way up the beach close to the grove of trees, so that the flames might be concealed by the overhanging cliffs and hills on either side, and thus, although there might be natives in the neighbourhood, we might escape being seen. We had got our wood ready to light when Sam and his companion came back.

"There's only one part, away to the left, where anybody, unless they've got wings, can come down," said Sam. "We must keep a look-out on it, and we shall have time, if many of the savages appear, to get the boat into the water and shove off before they can reach us. One of us had better keep guard there, and we shall be safe enough."

They had also discovered a waterfall, which came down over

the rock at an easily accessible spot, where we could fill the kettle we had brought with us. We accordingly spitted the fish which we had caught in the morning, though already they were not as fresh as we should have liked, and put on the kettle to boil, to make some tea which the missionary had given us. Following Sam's advice, we at once placed Jack Lizard on the look-out at the spot he had mentioned; we then cooked and ate our supper, and sent Tubb to relieve Jack. This done, we spread the boat's sail on the oars and boat-hook, to make an awning under which we could sleep; the sand was hot and dry enough so that we required no other bedding. It was arranged that we should relieve each other every two hours, and thus all might get a good spell of sleep. Had it not been for our anxiety about the schooner, we should have enjoyed our adventure. We had scarcely given a thought about ourselves, or what we should do, should we not find her. Our only idea had been to return to Mota; but from that island we were already at a considerable distance, and bad weather might come on before we could reach it. A few years before this, however, we should have been in much greater peril, for there would have been no place for which we could steer with any certainty of meeting with a friendly reception. It was sad to think that generation after generation had passed away, during which these beautiful islands had been inhabited by savages, to whom no one had carried the light of the Gospel; and that, even now, only on a few isolated spots were missionaries established, few of whom, owing to the numerous difficulties in their way, had made much progress.

As we had all been awake during the previous night, scarcely had we thrown ourselves on the sand than most of us were fast asleep. It appeared to me that I had scarcely closed my eyes when I was summoned by Charlie to keep my watch. Although I might have excused myself, as being in charge of the boat, I did not wish to do that. He told me that he had

W. H. G. Kingston

heard no sounds to indicate that any savages were in the neighbourhood. I took the musket which he handed me, and kept pacing up and down on the top of a bare mound, beyond which the ground sloped upwards towards the interior, as far as I could make out in the darkness. I thought it prudent, however, to cast my eye towards the other side of the bay, for it seemed to me that there was a way along under the cliffs at low water. It was arranged that should the sentry see any one coming, he was to shout to the rest of the party, who were to launch the boat, while he made the best of his way to join them. This might appear a very timid proceeding, but, considering the savage character of the natives, it was the only safe mode of showing them that we had no hostile intentions. We might thus also the better be able to gain their friendship.

Day broke while I was still on watch, and I could now distinguish the nature of the country. It was thickly wooded in all directions, with hills, or mountains, indeed, rising to a considerable elevation; and I was thankful, on looking at the grove, to see that the trees were loaded with cocoanuts. However, I would not quit my post till I was relieved, as it was far more important to keep a look-out now than it was during the night. Looking towards our camp, I saw Charlie on his feet, arousing the rest, and Dick soon joined me. I, of course, charged him to keep a vigilant look-out, but on no account to fire, even although the natives might appear with arms in their hands, and make threatening gestures when they saw him.

When I got back to the camp, Charlie proposed that we should push off and catch some fresh fish for breakfast, as the remainder of those we brought with us were no longer fit to eat. The boat accordingly shoved off with the four men and Charlie, while I remained on shore with the other musket in my hand, that I might be ready to assist Dick if necessary.

Much sooner than I expected, the boat returned with a sufficient number of mullet and bream to afford us food for the whole day. As we were all very hungry and I had made up the fire, we quickly cooked them, and I was just about to send Jack Lizard to relieve Dick, when the latter shouted—

"Here come some people; but there are only three or four fellows, and I cannot make out exactly who they are."

I quickly joined him, when I saw four men coming down the valley. Three of them were undoubtedly savages, but the fourth had some clothing on, and was taller and bigger than the others. He carried a huge knotted club in one hand, and a spear in the other. The rest of the men were also armed with spears. The first, from his dress and ornaments, was apparently a chief, but I was puzzled at his general appearance. On his getting nearer, though his skin was brown enough, I observed that it was very much lighter than that of his companions. Dick and I stood with the butts of our muskets on the ground, while we shook our handkerchiefs with our other hands. As the strangers got nearer, to my surprise the apparent chief shouted out—

"Hilloa! Who are you? What brings you here?"

"We came in to get water and fresh provisions," I answered. "And now I'd ask who you are."

"Why, as to that, I'm Prime Minister, High Priest, and Doctor Extraordinary to the king of this 'ere country," answered the man, who I now saw had been a white man, though certainly I could not call him so now.

"Very glad to meet you, friend; for some of the people in these parts are not very hospitable to strangers, and we have found it difficult to land to cook our food and stretch our

W. H. G. Kingston

legs, without the risk of being knocked on the head."

"Couldn't say, if I had not been with them, but what my people here might have treated you in the same way," answered the stranger, "Howsomedever, I will come and have a palaver with you, and hear the news, for I have not set eyes on any white chaps for I don't know how long."

Of course we told our new friend that we should be glad of his company, and he, followed by the blacks, went with us towards the boat.

"You don't happen to have any liquor aboard?" he asked. "It is a mighty long time since I have tasted a drop."

I was obliged to confess that we had no spirits, though we had still some of the tea the missionaries had given us. He looked much disappointed, and made a remark about the missionaries which I need not repeat. They were evidently not in his good graces.

He and his companions had seated themselves before the fire, when we gave them some tea sweetened with sugar, which seemed to their taste. They also condescended to eat the remainder of our fish, though the white man told us they were precious badly cooked. I saw Sam Pest looking at him while he was eating. At last Sam, seating himself by his side, said—

"Well, Dan Hogan, you seem to have forgotten me."

"No, I haven't, now you speak, though I do not know what I might have done if you had not opened your lips."

Though the two were old shipmates, they did not even shake hands, but sat eagerly talking together for some time, regardless of the rest of us. I could scarcely make out what they said. Sam, at last getting up, came towards me, and said—

"This 'ere old shipmate of mine has given me some news which you will be glad to hear for one thing, though not for another. The schooner has got safe into port, and is not far off from this."

"Safe!" I exclaimed, my heart bounding with joy, and I shouted the news to Charlie and the rest.

"Safe into port, but I did not say she was safe," said Sam. "In the first place, from what he tells me, she's carried away her mainmast, and seeing that she cannot put to sea, some of his black friends have made a plot to get hold of her, and if they do, they'll not leave any of those aboard alive. The captain, I know, keeps a sharp look-out; but they're cunning rascals, and will try, if they can, to circumvent him."

"How far off is she? How soon can we get there?" I asked eagerly. I could feel my heart beating as I spoke.

"He says about thirty miles, more or less, round the coast, though it is little more than a quarter of that distance across country."

"Then couldn't we go over land, and warn my brother?" I asked anxiously.

"Why, bless you, we should be knocked on the head by the first black fellows we might meet," answered Sam. "Our only chance is to go round by water, and I hope we may get there before any mischief is done."

"Then we have not a moment to lose," I exclaimed. "But we

must ask your friend to exert himself, and try to save them. Perhaps, when they hear that we are engaged in honest trading, they may be induced to abandon their design."

I spoke to Hogan, who, however, shook his head, as if he thought the attempt would be useless, though he promised to do what he could.

"You will understand, friend, that we shall be happy to reward you for any service you can render us, and you must point out to the natives that, should they commit any act of violence, they will be sure before long to be punished. British men-of-war are about to cruise in these parts for that very purpose, though, perhaps, the natives have never seen or heard of them as yet."

Hogan looked greatly astonished at hearing this, and exhibited some alarm himself. He promised, however, to tell the people, though he tried to persuade us that he could not be answerable for what they might do.

As every moment might be of importance, I wished him good-bye, and ordered the men to launch the boat. I observed that Sam parted from his old shipmate in a remarkably cold manner, as before, not even shaking hands with him. We immediately shoved off, Hogan and his companions standing on the beach, and watching us as we pulled out of the little bay, and soon afterwards I saw them going back by the way they had come. Hogan, I should have said, had minutely described the harbour in which the schooner lay, so that I had no fear about finding the place, if we could reach it before dark.

CHAPTER TEN

Nearly two hours of daylight had already gone by, and as there was at present a perfect calm, we should have to depend on our oars alone. I explained to the men that it was a matter of life and death to arrive as soon as possible.

"Never fear, Mr Ned," answered Jack Lizard. "We'll make the boat fly along as fast as our oars can send her."

As Dick had a sharp pair of eyes, I stationed him in the bows to look out for rocks; for, of course, to shorten the distance, we had to keep close to the land, or, rather, just outside the breakers, which, as we advanced, we found dashing on the shore. As we had had a good breakfast, we did not stop to dine, but Charlie handed round a mug of water, that the men might moisten their lips. As I sat in the stern-sheets holding the yoke-lines, I felt as if I was steering in a race; and so it was—a race against the machinations of the treacherous savages; but I trusted that we should win, and be in time to warn Harry of their evil intentions. I was pleased with the way the men behaved, evidently exerting their strength to the utmost, and even old Sam did not utter a complaint. As we pulled on, I eagerly looked out for each point or headland, hoping that it might be the one beyond which we should find the harbour.

W. H. G. Kingston

Everywhere the country was covered with trees. Sometimes there were cliffs, and at others the land rose in bold slopes almost from the water's edge; but nowhere did we see any coral reefs. This was owing, Charlie said, to the existence of a volcano, which we observed somewhere in the interior, sending forth clouds of smoke and ashes, occasionally bright flames darting up, though scarcely visible in the sunlight. The lava, he said, rolled down into the sea, and so heated the water that it prevented the existence of the coral insects. Here and there were small sandy bays, in which canoes were drawn up. On observing them, I feared that some might come off and interfere with us. However, our boat was so small an object, and being without a sail, the natives probably scarcely observed her as we glided rapidly by. Perhaps they might have taken her for some marine monster, or other fish which had just risen above the surface. Occasionally we had to cross a broad bay, when we were, in consequence, at a considerable distance from the land; but I took care to examine it carefully, so as to be sure that the harbour we were searching for was not within it.

Night was drawing on. We had been pulling, we calculated, for not less than seven hours, and must have been going at the rate of four knots an hour. Charlie thought that there might have been a current against us, or, perhaps, we had scarcely made good the four knots as I supposed, or else that the distance was greater than Hogan had told us. As yet, however, we had seen no indication of an opening. A tree-covered point was before us; we steered for it.

"Perhaps we shall find the harbour on the other side," said Charlie.

The men had not lately been pulling as fast as in the early part of the day; and no wonder, for their arms were becoming weary with their exertions. Still they went on.

"Never fear, sir," cried Jack Lizard. "We've got some go in us yet. Cheer up, lads, cheer up; let us give way with a will again."

The point was rounded when we saw what Charlie and I felt nearly sure was the entrance to the harbour. We were already steering for it when we made out half a dozen canoes, which had just rounded the opposite point, and soon came paddling towards us. They might have had no unfriendly intentions; but, at all events, we were anxious not to encounter them. As we pulled on, we became perfectly convinced, by the appearance of the land, that we had discovered the harbour we were in search of. The canoes were coming up with us, and it seemed doubtful whether we should get into the harbour before them. Our men, though they had previously appeared too much fatigued to pull longer, redoubled their efforts, and point after point was passed, when at length I was gladdened by the sight of the schooner at anchor.

I raised a shout of joy. "Hurrah, hurrah! There she is!" I exclaimed.

"And there are the canoes!" cried Jack Lizard. "But we'll be alongside her before they're up with us."

Harry, who was on deck, saw us coming, and presently Mary and Fanny came up, and Nat, and waved to us. We were quickly on board, and rapidly exchanging accounts with each other. Harry had been as anxious about us as we had been about him, for, as he could not tell whether we had put off from Mota before squall came on, he feared that we might have been exposed to its fury.

The canoes, seeing us safe on board, turned aside and paddled for the shore. Whether or not they had had any intention of attacking the boat, this showed us that they believed the schooner was able to defend us.

Harry said that he had been compelled to be very strict with them, although he had hitherto remained on good terms. He had held to his rule of allowing only a few men to come on board at a time, and he had made these leave their arms in the canoes, while, as soon as evening drew on, he compelled all on board to return to the shore. When I told him of the warning Hogan had given us, he replied that he had brought the natives into such good order that he did not think they would attempt any act of treachery.

"That is just what Sam was afraid of," I observed. "Their object, by pretending to be quiet and friendly, is to throw us off our guard. However, now that the schooner's crew is strengthened by our arrival, perhaps they'll abandon their designs."

He told me that he had been arranging with a chief for leave to cut down a tree from which to make a mainmast. "It will take some time," he continued, "but it must be done, and as the natives cannot cut down the tree, we must manage to do it ourselves. It did occur to me that, while we were thus engaged, they might think it a favourable opportunity to attack us, unless we are on our guard."

"From what Hogan told Sam, we were much afraid that they might attempt to cut you off even before our arrival," I observed. "The old sailor had, by some means or other, gained intelligence of their designs, although he acknowledged that he was very uncertain whether he should be able to put you on your guard in time to save you."

"One thing is positive, that we cannot leave this harbour till we have obtained a mast. And we must have it, therefore, at all risks," said Harry.

"I advise that we should get hold of a chief, or some other person of influence, and keep him as a hostage on board, while our people are working on shore," said Charlie Tilston. "The wildest savages know what that means, and will not venture to attack us while we have a chief in our power."

"A capital idea!" said Harry; "but the question is, how are we to bell the cat, or rather, get hold of a chief?"

"I will go on shore with Sam Pest, and try to induce one of them to come off," said Charlie. "It would be useless to take either the New Zealander or the Sandwich Island man, as neither of them speak a word of the language of these people, but Sam can make himself understood."

Harry thought that there was much risk in the undertaking, but Sam, when told of the plan, was ready enough to go, and I begged that I might accompany Charlie, as I did not like the idea of his going alone. We were all to be well armed, and to be on the watch to prevent any savage from getting behind us—this, should they have any treacherous intentions, they were sure to attempt doing. Charlie proposed carrying a few articles to present to the chief, with the promise of others, in exchange for provisions and such things as we should require, if he would come to receive them. This was considered more politic than carrying on the trading first, and promising the presents afterwards, as the chief might doubt whether they would be delivered. From what we gleaned from Sam, they had more than once before been tricked by white men, who had come into their harbour, and were therefore likely to be suspicious of our intentions.

As soon as the plan was arranged, Charlie and I, with Sam, Jack Lizard, and two other men, shoved off and pulled for the shore. As we approached, we found a number of savages armed with clubs, collected on the beach. We pulled slowly, looking out for one who, from the ornaments he wore, and his general appearance, might prove to be a chief.

"That's the fellow we want," said Charlie, pointing out a man who wore an ornamented head-dress and breastplate, with a necklace and rings round his arms. We waved, and made signs to him to approach, and we steered the boat directly towards where he stood. Charlie then held up several articles he had brought. The chief seemed to understand our object, and ordering his people to stand back, he advanced without hesitation. We accordingly ran in the boat; Charlie and Sam stepped on shore, while Jack Lizard and I sat with our muskets in our hands, ready to cover them should they be attacked. Charlie then presented first one article and then another, and Sam tried to explain, as far as his knowledge of the language would allow him, our object to the chief, who seemed highly pleased, and stepping back, exhibited the gifts he had received to his attendants. Sam then gave him to understand that we had many more of the same description on board. At first, I was afraid that he would not consent to accompany us; but at length his cupidity overcame his fears, and Sam, advising him to come lest others should obtain the goods we had to dispose of, he stepped into the boat.

As it was evident that she could not well carry more than one person besides ourselves, Sam made signs to the others that we could not take them on board, and at once pulled away from the beach. This showed the savages that we had not come for the purpose of kidnapping them. The chief, however, looked somewhat nervous, and I was afraid might, after all, jump overboard, and swim back to the shore. I told Charlie, therefore, to try and occupy his attention by showing him some of the other articles which we had brought. What interested him most was a telescope, through which, having adjusted the focus, we made him look at his friends. He almost let it drop in his astonishment at seeing them so near, and had not Charlie held it, it would have fallen overboard. He looked through it again and again, each time expressing by signs his wonder, and of course utterly unable to comprehend how the objects he saw through it were brought so near. I was very glad when we got him safe alongside.

Stepping on deck, he gazed about him with almost as much astonishment as he had exhibited when looking through the telescope. Harry stood ready to receive him, and told Sam to say how happy he was to have him come on board. We then showed him some of the articles which we had brought for trading, and gave him to understand that a certain number of them should be his, as soon as the mast was ready. Sam also was told to explain to him that till then he must remain on board, and that, should his countrymen offer any violence to our people, he would be the sufferer. He seemed to understand this perfectly well. The difficulty, however, was to let the natives know why we had carried him off, as we could not allow him to return to tell them so. The only way of accomplishing our object was to bring off one or two more natives, who might convey any message he desired to send. After some persuasion, we induced him to go down to a spare space in the hold, when some food likely to suit his taste was placed before him, and the mate and Dick sat down to eat with him.

As soon as they were thus engaged, Charlie and I shoved off, and pulled for the shore. At first the natives, though they had been eager to accompany their chief, seemed unwilling to embark; but at last we persuaded two to trust themselves with us. On pulling back we amused them as we had the chief, and as soon as they got on board we conducted them down below. We placed some food before them, and when their meal was over, we got Sam to try and explain to them that we intended to keep their chief as a hostage, while our people were on shore cutting down the tree; that he would be

W. H. G. Kingston

well treated, and ample payment made to him. They seemed to understand this clearly, and after they had had a conversation with the chief, we told them that we would convey them back to the shore. They appeared to be in no way dissatisfied with the arrangement, and willingly got into the boat, leaving their chief on board.

"Please, sir, we must keep a sharp look-out on that chap," observed Sam, "or maybe he'll jump overboard and swim ashore."

"He'll lose the goods we promised him if he does," said Harry.

"But he does not think so; for he knows the schooner cannot get away, and he expects to take her some dark night, then to get hold of everything on board."

"We will not stand on any ceremony with him, then, but keep him safely under hatches till we get the mast aboard," said Harry.

We at once landed the two natives, who explained to the rest our object in keeping the chief. This did not appear to surprise them, nor did they show any unfriendly feeling towards us, but continued to bring down fresh provisions, till we gave them to understand that we had as much as we wanted. As there was no time to be lost, the carpenter, and men to assist him, at once went on shore to cut down the tree. Charlie and I accompanied them to superintend the operation. Notwithstanding the pacific behaviour of the natives, we considered it prudent to go well armed, and to keep a vigilant watch all the time on their movements. As the tree we required was not a large one, it was quickly cut down, and the branches and bark being chopped off, we commenced dragging it towards the water. None of the natives, however, offered to assist us. We had got to within about a hundred yards of the beach, when we saw a number of natives collecting on either side, with clubs and spears in their hands; and at the same time we observed, to our dismay, a fleet of canoes paddling towards the schooner. We had too much reason to fear that a simultaneous attack was to be made on us and her. Providentially, our boat, which lay hauled up on the beach, had not been touched, and we determined therefore to make a rush for her, and to try and reach the schooner before the canoes could get alongside, as, if once on board, we might hope to defend her against any number of assailants.

"Whatever we do, let us keep together," cried Charlie.

Presenting our muskets at the natives, we ordered them to keep back, and while he and I retreated with our faces towards them, the men rushed on to launch the boat. Still the savages well knew that after we had discharged our pieces we should be defenceless. They hesitated, however, no one wishing to be shot, and we were able to get the boat off and to leap into her. Still it seemed very doubtful whether we could gain the schooner before the canoes. Scarcely, however, had we shoved off from the shore, when I caught sight of a white sail appearing over the point which formed the southern entrance to the harbour, and almost immediately afterwards a large vessel appeared, steering directly for it. The natives saw her; her appearance evidently disconcerted them, for, instead of continuing their course towards the schooner, they paddled away for the shore.

The breeze being fair, the stranger came rapidly on, and, shortening sail, brought up a short distance outside where the *Dainty* lay. Harry immediately sent me alongside to tell her captain what had occurred. I found that she was a whaler, which had put in for fresh provisions and water. As she

W. H. G. Kingston

carried four guns and a numerous crew, the captain said that he had no fear of the natives; besides which, he well knew how to deal them, though he confessed that he might have been deceived had we not warned him of their treacherous conduct. The first thing to be done was to get off the spar intended for our mast. He accordingly sent a couple of boats well armed to assist us, and lent us his carpenters, who quickly shaped it as it was required. Our captive chief, on being told of the meditated attack of his countrymen, looked very much alarmed, believing that we should in consequence put him to death. We gave him to understand that we had no intention of doing so, and that, as we had obtained the spar, we would pay him and send him on shore, hoping that he would induce his countrymen to behave in a friendly way to white men in future. This, as far as we could understand, he promised faithfully to do. Landing him on the beach, we shook hands, and let him go his way with the goods he had obtained. Next morning, he and a number of his people appeared, loaded with provisions of all sorts, and before the day was over the whaler obtained as much as she required. The natives kept at a respectful distance during the time her boats crews were filling the casks with water. With the assistance of the captain of the whaler we got our mast stepped and rigged, and both vessels sailed together.

We heard nothing more during our stay of Hogan, or what had become of him. Probably he fell a victim to the jealousy of the natives—a common fate of so many white men who have abandoned themselves to a savage life. Parting from the whaler, we made the best of our way to Sydney, where Harry immediately gave information to the authorities of the piratical cruise of the *Wasp*.

Having disposed of our cargo, we returned to Brisbane, where we found that everything had been going on in a satisfactory manner.

Charles Tilston, instead of going home, resolved to settle there, and, as I had long suspected would be the case, made an offer to Fanny Amiel, who accepted him.

Dick and I, with old Tom Platt and Jack Lizard, made several successful trips in the *Dainty*; but our sisters-in-law agreed that interesting as had been their voyage, they did not wish ever to make another. I need not say the adventures we met with have often since served us as subjects of conversation, and I hope that we were all grateful for our preservation from the many dangers we encountered.

I must confess, before I conclude, that I was induced to write the narrative of our voyage, not merely to amuse my readers, but to interest them in the dark-skinned inhabitants of the almost countless beautiful islands spread over the Pacific, and to induce them to give their warm support to the missionary efforts now making to convey the blessed light of the gospel to those savage races so long plunged in the utter darkness of heathenism. A wonderful work has already been accomplished. Thousands and tens of thousands of the Pacific Islanders have become civilised and enlightened; but much—very much—remains to be done, and I would remind my readers that they should consider it a privilege to help with their subscriptions to send men forth who are willing to engage in the noble and glorious undertaking.

THE END

W. H. G. Kingston

ABOUT THE AUTHOR

William Henry Giles Kingston (1814 - 1880), writer of tales for boys, born in London, but spent much of his youth in Oporto, where his father was a merchant.

His first book, The Circassian Chief, appeared in 1844. His first book for boys, Peter the Whaler, was published in 1851, and had such success that he retired from business and devoted himself entirely to the production of this kind of literature, in which his popularity was deservedly great; and during 30 years he wrote upwards of 130 tales, including The Three Midshipmen (1862), The Three Lieutenants (1874), The Three Commanders (1875), The Three Admirals (1877), Digby Heathcote, etc.

He also conducted various papers, including The Colonist, and Colonial Magazine and East India Review. He was also interested in emigration, volunteering, and various philanthropic schemes. For services in negotiating a commercial treaty with Portugal he received a Portuguese knighthood, and for his literary labours a Government pension.

Choose from Thousands of 1stWorldLibrary Classics By

A. M. Barnard
Ada Leverson
Adolphus William Ward
Aesop
Agatha Christie
Alexander Aaronsohn
Alexander Kielland
Alexandre Dumas
Alfred Gatty
Alfred Ollivant
Alice Duer Miller
Alice Turner Curtis
Alice Dunbar
Allen Chapman
Alleyne Ireland
Ambrose Bierce
Amelia E. Barr
Amory H. Bradford
Andrew Lang
Andrew McFarland Davis
Andy Adams
Angela Brazil
Anna Alice Chapin
Anna Sewell
Annie Besant
Annie Hamilton Donnell
Annie Payson Call
Annie Roe Carr
Annonaymous
Anton Chekhov
Archibald Lee Fletcher
Arnold Bennett
Arthur C. Benson
Arthur Conan Doyle
Arthur M. Winfield
Arthur Ransome
Arthur Schnitzler
Arthur Train
Atticus
B.H. Baden-Powell
B. M. Bower
B. C. Chatterjee
Baroness Emmuska Orczy
Baroness Orczy
Basil King
Bayard Taylor
Ben Macomber
Bertha Muzzy Bower
Bjornstjerne Bjornson

Booth Tarkington
Boyd Cable
Bram Stoker
C. Collodi
C. E. Orr
C. M. Ingleby
Carolyn Wells
Catherine Parr Traill
Charles A. Eastman
Charles Amory Beach
Charles Dickens
Charles Dudley Warner
Charles Farrar Browne
Charles Ives
Charles Kingsley
Charles Klein
Charles Hanson Towne
Charles Lathrop Pack
Charles Romyn Dake
Charles Whibley
Charles Willing Beale
Charlotte M. Braeme
Charlotte M. Yonge
Charlotte Perkins Stetson
Clair W. Hayes
Clarence Day Jr.
Clarence E. Mulford
Clemence Housman
Confucius
Coningsby Dawson
Cornelis DeWitt Wilcox
Cyril Burleigh
D. H. Lawrence
Daniel Defoe
David Garnett
Dinah Craik
Don Carlos Janes
Donald Keyhoe
Dorothy Kilner
Dougan Clark
Douglas Fairbanks
E. Nesbit
E. P. Roe
E. Phillips Oppenheim
E. S. Brooks
Earl Barnes
Edgar Rice Burroughs
Edith Van Dyne
Edith Wharton

Edward Everett Hale
Edward J. O'Biren
Edward S. Ellis
Edwin L. Arnold
Eleanor Atkins
Eleanor Hallowell Abbott
Eliot Gregory
Elizabeth Gaskell
Elizabeth McCracken
Elizabeth Von Arnim
Ellem Key
Emerson Hough
Emilie F. Carlen
Emily Bronte
Emily Dickinson
Enid Bagnold
Enilor Macartney Lane
Erasmus W. Jones
Ernie Howard Pie
Ethel May Dell
Ethel Turner
Ethel Watts Mumford
Eugene Sue
Eugenie Foa
Eugene Wood
Eustace Hale Ball
Evelyn Everett-green
Everard Cotes
F. H. Cheley
F. J. Cross
F. Marion Crawford
Fannie E. Newberry
Federick Austin Ogg
Ferdinand Ossendowski
Fergus Hume
Florence A. Kilpatrick
Fremont B. Deering
Francis Bacon
Francis Darwin
Frances Hodgson Burnett
Frances Parkinson Keyes
Frank Gee Patchin
Frank Harris
Frank Jewett Mather
Frank L. Packard
Frank V. Webster
Frederic Stewart Isham
Frederick Trevor Hill
Frederick Winslow Taylor

Friedrich Kerst
Friedrich Nietzsche
Fyodor Dostoyevsky
G.A. Henty
G.K. Chesterton
Gabrielle E. Jackson
Garrett P. Serviss
Gaston Leroux
George A. Warren
George Ade
Geroge Bernard Shaw
George Cary Eggleston
George Durston
George Ebers
George Eliot
George Gissing
George MacDonald
George Meredith
George Orwell
George Sylvester Viereck
George Tucker
George W. Cable
George Wharton James
Gertrude Atherton
Gordon Casserly
Grace E. King
Grace Gallatin
Grace Greenwood
Grant Allen
Guillermo A. Sherwell
Gulielma Zollinger
Gustav Flaubert
H. A. Cody
H. B. Irving
H.C. Bailey
H. G. Wells
H. H. Munro
H. Irving Hancock
H. R. Naylor
H. Rider Haggard
H. W. C. Davis
Haldeman Julius
Hall Caine
Hamilton Wright Mabie
Hans Christian Andersen
Harold Avery
Harold McGrath
Harriet Beecher Stowe
Harry Castlemon
Harry Coghill
Harry Houidini

Hayden Carruth
Helent Hunt Jackson
Helen Nicolay
Hendrik Conscience
Hendy David Thoreau
Henri Barbusse
Henrik Ibsen
Henry Adams
Henry Ford
Henry Frost
Henry James
Henry Jones Ford
Henry Seton Merriman
Henry W Longfellow
Herbert A. Giles
Herbert Carter
Herbert N. Casson
Herman Hesse
Hildegard G. Frey
Homer
Honore De Balzac
Horace B. Day
Horace Walpole
Horatio Alger Jr.
Howard Pyle
Howard R. Garis
Hugh Lofting
Hugh Walpole
Humphry Ward
Ian Maclaren
Inez Haynes Gillmore
Irving Bacheller
Isabel Cecilia Williams
Isabel Hornibrook
Israel Abrahams
Ivan Turgenev
J.G.Austin
J. Henri Fabre
J. M. Barrie
J. M. Walsh
J. Macdonald Oxley
J. R. Miller
J. S. Fletcher
J. S. Knowles
J. Storer Clouston
J. W. Duffield
Jack London
Jacob Abbott
James Allen
James Andrews
James Baldwin

James Branch Cabell
James DeMille
James Joyce
James Lane Allen
James Lane Allen
James Oliver Curwood
James Oppenheim
James Otis
James R. Driscoll
Jane Abbott
Jane Austen
Jane L. Stewart
Janet Aldridge
Jens Peter Jacobsen
Jerome K. Jerome
Jessie Graham Flower
John Buchan
John Burroughs
John Cournos
John F. Kennedy
John Gay
John Glasworthy
John Habberton
John Joy Bell
John Kendrick Bangs
John Milton
John Philip Sousa
John Taintor Foote
Jonas Lauritz Idemil Lie
Jonathan Swift
Joseph A. Altsheler
Joseph Carey
Joseph Conrad
Joseph E. Badger Jr
Joseph Hergesheimer
Joseph Jacobs
Jules Vernes
Julian Hawthrone
Julie A Lippmann
Justin Huntly McCarthy
Kakuzo Okakura
Karle Wilson Baker
Kate Chopin
Kenneth Grahame
Kenneth McGaffey
Kate Langley Bosher
Kate Langley Bosher
Katherine Cecil Thurston
Katherine Stokes
L. A. Abbot
L. T. Meade

L. Frank Baum
Latta Griswold
Laura Dent Crane
Laura Lee Hope
Laurence Housman
Lawrence Beasley
Leo Tolstoy
Leonid Andreyev
Lewis Carroll
Lewis Sperry Chafer
Lilian Bell
Lloyd Osbourne
Louis Hughes
Louis Joseph Vance
Louis Tracy
Louisa May Alcott
Lucy Fitch Perkins
Lucy Maud Montgomery
Luther Benson
Lydia Miller Middleton
Lyndon Orr
M. Corvus
M. H. Adams
Margaret E. Sangster
Margret Howth
Margaret Vandercook
Margaret W. Hungerford
Margret Penrose
Maria Edgeworth
Maria Thompson Daviess
Mariano Azuela
Marion Polk Angellotti
Mark Overton
Mark Twain
Mary Austin
Mary Catherine Crowley
Mary Cole
Mary Hastings Bradley
Mary Roberts Rinehart
Mary Rowlandson
M. Wollstonecraft Shelley
Maud Lindsay
Max Beerbohm
Myra Kelly
Nathaniel Hawthrone
Nicolo Machiavelli
O. F. Walton
Oscar Wilde

Owen Johnson
P.G. Wodehouse
Paul and Mabel Thorne
Paul G. Tomlinson
Paul Severing
Percy Brebner
Percy Keese Fitzhugh
Peter B. Kyne
Plato
Quincy Allen
R. Derby Holmes
R. L. Stevenson
R. S. Ball
Rabindranath Tagore
Rahul Alvares
Ralph Bonehill
Ralph Henry Barbour
Ralph Victor
Ralph Waldo Emmerson
Rene Descartes
Ray Cummings
Rex Beach
Rex E. Beach
Richard Harding Davis
Richard Jefferies
Richard Le Gallienne
Robert Barr
Robert Frost
Robert Gordon Anderson
Robert L. Drake
Robert Lansing
Robert Lynd
Robert Michael Ballantyne
Robert W. Chambers
Rosa Nouchette Carey
Rudyard Kipling
Saint Augustine
Samuel B. Allison
Samuel Hopkins Adams
Sarah Bernhardt
Sarah C. Hallowell
Selma Lagerlof
Sherwood Anderson
Sigmund Freud
Standish O'Grady
Stanley Weyman
Stella Benson
Stella M. Francis

Stephen Crane
Stewart Edward White
Stijn Streuvels
Swami Abhedananda
Swami Parmananda
T. S. Ackland
T. S. Arthur
The Princess Der Ling
Thomas A. Janvier
Thomas A Kempis
Thomas Anderton
Thomas Bailey Aldrich
Thomas Bulfinch
Thomas De Quincey
Thomas Dixon
Thomas H. Huxley
Thomas Hardy
Thomas More
Thornton W. Burgess
U. S. Grant
Upton Sinclair
Valentine Williams
Various Authors
Vaughan Kester
Victor Appleton
Victor G. Durham
Victoria Cross
Virginia Woolf
Wadsworth Camp
Walter Camp
Walter Scott
Washington Irving
Wilbur Lawton
Wilkie Collins
Willa Cather
Willard F. Baker
William Dean Howells
William le Queux
W. Makepeace Thackeray
William W. Walter
William Shakespeare
Winston Churchill
Yei Theodora Ozaki
Yogi Ramacharaka
Young E. Allison
Zane Grey

www.ingramcontent.com/pod-product-compliance
Lightning Source LLC
Chambersburg PA
CBHW051840170626
46807CB00003B/1277